THE GALLANT
BOYS OF
GETTYSBURG

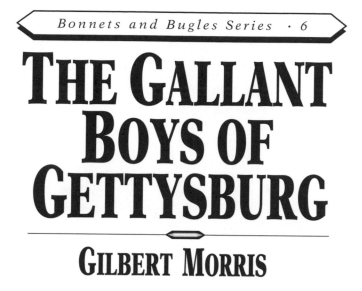

Bonnets and Bugles Series · 6

THE GALLANT BOYS OF GETTYSBURG

GILBERT MORRIS

MOODY PRESS
CHICAGO

ISBN: 0-8024-0916-7

3 5 7 9 10 8 6 4 2

Printed in the United States of America

To Staci—my granddaughter
You owe me a hug and a kiss for this dedication!

Contents

1
An Urgent Plea

Be still, Daisy! I'm sick and tired of fooling with you!"

Leah Carter, seated on a three-legged stool, slapped the glossy hide of the surprised Daisy, who turned to look at her and utter a long, low moo.

Leah endured the gaze of the enormous brown eyes of her favorite cow, then sighed heavily. Patting Daisy's heaving side, she said, "I'm sorry, Daisy—it's not your fault. I'm just not fit to live with today."

A rebellious expression on her face, she leaned her head against Daisy's flank and began milking again. Streams of white liquid drummed into the tin bucket, and soon frothy milk half filled the pail.

"That's enough for now. You'll need the rest of your milk for Suky." Daisy nodded her head as if in agreement, and Leah stroked the animal fondly between the horns.

"I'll bet if it were *your* birthday," Leah muttered, "Suky wouldn't forget it." Again Daisy mooed sympathetically—or so Leah took it. Her lips pursed, and she touched the curving horns for a moment, then whispered, "It's pretty bad, Daisy, to have your fifteenth birthday and not a single soul even notices it!"

She opened the gate, and Daisy ambled out of the stall, where she was greeted enthusiastically by her calf. Suky at once began having his evening meal. Leah watched for a moment, then picked up the bucket and started for the house.

Leah was a tall girl—too tall, she thought, calling herself "tall and gawky." Actually she was not gawky, though she was taller than most girls her age. She wore a pair of faded blue overalls that had once belonged to her brother, Royal, and noted that she was beginning to fill them out more than she had the previous year.

Her eyes were an odd color, sometimes seeming to be light green but at other times light blue. A relative who had been to sea once remarked, "Your eyes are just the blue-green color of the ocean at certain times of the year, Leah." Her braids, a rich blonde, came down almost to her waist. Leah was an attractive young woman—and on her fifteenth birthday she had hoped someone might even tell her so.

Reaching the fence that surrounded the barn, she slipped through the gate muttering, "At least somebody could say, 'Happy birthday,' you'd think!" Leah kicked at Max, the black-and-white shepherd dog that came loping up to greet her with his red tongue lolling. Her foot merely grazed him, but he let out a yelp and backed away, eyeing her cautiously.

"Get away from me, Max!" she said and then at once felt terrible. The two were very close, and she at once bent over saying, "I'm sorry, Max. Here. You can kick me if you want to—or bite me."

Max clearly had no desire to do either of those things. Being reassured by the note in her voice, he came forward again, tail wagging furiously. He licked her face, and, in an effort to get away, Leah stepped into a slight hole in the ground.

"Noooo!" she cried, finding herself falling. She tried to balance the milk, but as she went down full length, it sloshed down the front of her overalls. "That does it!" she muttered and threw the bucket blindly as far as she could.

"Whoa! What's going on, Leah?"

Leah looked up to see Ezra Payne, who had approached without her noticing and now came running. He put a hand out, saying, "Here, let me help you up."

"I can get up by myself!"

Leah scrambled to her feet and felt her face flush with embarrassment. She stared at the boy defiantly. "Well, go on and laugh. I can see you want to."

Ezra Payne was seventeen with warm brown eyes and mahogany colored hair. Since he had come to live with the Carters, the two had grown to be very good friends. Ezra could never forget that she had practically saved his life.

Ezra had escaped from a Confederate prison camp close to Richmond, and it was Leah who found him almost dead with fever. She hid him on her uncle's farm and, along with Jeff Majors, arranged his escape. Ezra was an orphan with no family at all and had been glad to stay on and work for Leah's parents as a hired hand.

Leah was usually good-tempered, but now her brows were pulled down in a frown, her lips in a thin white line. She seemed to be daring him to laugh.

Ezra hesitated, then protested, "Why, I wasn't laughing." He brought back the bucket, saying mildly, "Everybody falls down once in a while."

Leah wanted to snap at him. She had already lashed out at Daisy and at Max—but that had not been very satisfactory. She had carefully hinted to Ezra more than two weeks earlier that her birthday was on June 15. Yet he had not said one word. But then, neither had anyone else! She said almost bitterly, "The older I get, the clumsier I get."

She started toward the house.

Ezra walked along by her side. He acted almost afraid to speak. He was a mild-mannered young Northerner, and living in Kentucky had been a trial for him. Leah knew that. He had learned that Southerners had a great deal of pride, and now Leah, angry and with the front of her overalls soaked with milk, must have looked rather formidable.

"Well," he said cheerfully at last, "your pa'll be back pretty soon, and maybe you and me can go with him on another trip to take stuff to the soldiers."

Leah's father was a sutler. He sold supplies and Bibles to the soldiers of the Union army. Leah had gone with him on earlier trips and so had Ezra. Ordinarily the thought of such a trip would have pleased her, but she said stiffly, "I don't want to go out on any old wagon."

Actually she would love to do that very thing, for following the army had been adventurous and a great deal of excitement. Her father believed that God had called him to distribute Bibles and tracts to the troops, and Leah had thrown herself into this work with a great deal of pleasure. Now, however, she was upset and simply shook the braids that hung down her back in an angry gesture and walked up the front steps.

Ezra followed close behind her. "I think we're gonna have fresh pork chops for supper."

"I don't want any old pork chops!"

She marched into the house and started for her room, but her mother called, "Leah, come into the dining room, please."

Rebelliously Leah shot a glance at Ezra, who was standing watching her. Then she flounced down the hall and into the large dining room, expecting to see her mother.

"Happy birthday! Surprise! Surprise!"

Leah stopped as abruptly as if she had run into a wall. The dining room was packed with people. With a startled gaze, she saw a huge cake sitting in the middle of the table, while on each side were piled colorfully wrapped gifts. Her mother stood behind the table along with her nineteen-year-old sister, Sarah. Sarah's arm was around ten-year-old Morena. Several neighbors were there, including the sons and daughters of the families that lived close, and Leah felt absolutely awful.

Ezra came in to stand beside her. He grinned broadly, catching her eye. "Well, you're all dressed up for your birthday party, Leah."

Leah looked down at her faded, ragged blue overalls soaked with milk, and she blushed. "This is awful!" she said.

She turned to go, but Ezra caught her by the arm and held on. "What's wrong?" he asked. "You look all right to me."

Mary Carter, Leah's mother, stepped out from behind the table. "This was mean," she said, but there was a smile on her lips. "But we wanted to surprise you."

"Well, you surprised me all right," Leah said ruefully. She felt ashamed of the way she had been acting and managed a smile. "Let me go change clothes, and I'll be right back."

She ran back to her room, but when she opened the door and stepped inside she stopped abruptly. There on the bed was the most beautiful dress she had ever seen. It was light green with small white flowers, and it was made of silk. Leah knew her mother had made it, laboring over it secretly, and she squealed with delight. Stripping off her old overalls, she quickly washed her face at the washstand, then slipped into the dress.

Now she saw at the bedside a pair of brand-new shoes, the ones she had longed for for a long time, high-topped, light tan shoes with high heels. She pulled on stockings, then put on the shoes and quickly arranged her hair in front of the mirror. She was shocked at how mature she looked in the new dress. And it fit perfectly!

The party was a complete success. Besides the new dress from her mother and the shoes from Sarah, there were smaller gifts from the others. One that took her breath away was handed to her by Ezra. It felt heavy, and with excitement she pulled the paper off. When it was peeled away, she took a deep breath and said, "Ezra, it's beautiful!"

It was a wooden box made of walnut, exquisite-ly carved and finished with a high sheen. She lifted the lid and saw that the inside was lined with green felt. When she looked up, Leah's eyes were glowing. "It's beautiful!" she repeated.

"You can keep all your jewelry in there," Ezra said, rather embarrassed.

One of the boys from the next farm grinned. "Or all those love letters you get from Jeff."

A laugh went around the room, and Leah flushed. She stroked the lid of the box and said, "We always had our birthdays together—Jeff and me—before the Majorses left for Virginia."

Sarah came over and put her arm around her younger sister. Sarah was a beautiful girl. She had dark hair, dark blue eyes, and a creamy complexion. She said, "You'll have your birthdays together again when this war's over."

The mention of the war threatened to dampen everyone's spirits, and Mrs. Carter quickly said, "Now, let's have some more ice cream. Ezra, you can turn the crank."

When the party was over and everyone was gone, Leah sat on the front porch with Ezra. The two had been quiet for some time, and finally Ezra said, "Have you heard from Jeff lately?"

"I got a letter two weeks ago."

"What did he say?"

"He said he thought there'd be more fighting soon." She turned to face him and shook her head. "I worry so much about him—and about Royal."

Ezra had given his parole not to return to the Union army, but Leah knew he remembered some of the terrors and hardships of the war.

He said, "Well, I guess all we can do is pray for them."

Leah reached over and patted his hand. "Yes," she whispered, "I guess that's all we can do."

Sarah was standing at the window when a tall, rangy man on a tall, rangy mule pulled up in front of the gate. A smile touched her lips. She had always thought that Pete Mangus and his mule resembled each other a great deal. Pete carried the mail in the mountains close to Pineville, Kentucky.

Sarah hurried out to meet him. The sun was high in the sky, and this spring of 1863 had been the mildest that people in Pineville could remember. "Hello, Pete," she said. "You have some mail for us?"

"Shore do." Pete fumbled in the leather bag slung over the mule's shoulders and came up with a small packet of letters. He shuffled through them and nodded. "Got two. One's from your pa, looks like. And the other is the one you been looking for, I reckon." Pete grinned down at her and handed her the letters. "That young Rebel you're so sweet on shore keeps the mail hot, don't he? But you was sweet on him before him and his family left to go South."

Sarah sometimes got upset with Pete, who felt that his status as mailman enabled him to know all the private business that went on between those who exchanged letters. However, everyone in the valley knew that she and Tom Majors had been, as Pete put it, "sweet on each other" before the war. Now, however, Tom was in the Confederate army, and her own brother was in the Union army. A great problem, but that's the way it was.

She longed to open the letter from Tom at once but knew that Pete would demand to know exactly what it said, so she said, "Stop on your way back, and I'll give you some of the gingerbread I'm making."

"Shore will!"

Sarah hurried into the house and opened Tom's letter, which was brief. Sitting at the kitchen table, she read it slowly, savoring every word. As she read, she could see Tom's face. He was tall and dark and handsome like his father, Nelson Majors, a Confederate captain, and like his brother, Jeff, who was a drummer boy in the same army.

Sarah's lips grew tight, for Tom wrote of the hardships that the people of the South were enduring. She knew he did not do this to arouse pity but simply to relate the facts. He did not mention the fighting that was to come, but her heart contracted as she realized that a young man in the Confederate army—or the Union army for that matter—had little chance of escaping without at least being wounded.

The last paragraph said,

> I love you more than I ever did, Sarah. I'd give anything if we could get married and raise a family. I know that can't be, the way things are, but I can keep hoping anyway. Don't forget me.
>
> Love, Tom

Sarah put the letter down and sat for a long time staring at it. There was a sadness in her that she could not contain. Finally, with a sigh, she folded the letter and picked up the other one. It was not from her father.

She did not recognize the handwriting at first, and when she opened the letter she looked at once at the signature at the bottom of the page. "Abigail!" she whispered and smiled. But when she began to read, the smile left her face almost instantly.

Abigail Smith had been her best friend since early childhood. She had married a young man

17

from the North named Albert Munson. It had been one of the saddest moments of Sarah's life when her friend moved away to Pennsylvania. Now as she read Abigail's letter, lines appeared around her eyes as she frowned at the fine script:

Dear Sarah,

You'll be glad to hear that I am going to have a baby. You remember how much we always talked about how nice it would be to have a baby to take care of—well, Al and I are very happy to announce that we're going to be a mother and a father.

But I must also tell you something else, Sarah. I've tried not complain since I've been here, but I've been so lonely. I was spoiled when I was home, and here I've had rather a hard time. Albert has been gone with his regiment, and he has almost no family. I have met several people and have tried to make friends, but the Northern people here are suspicious because I come from the South.

What I'm trying to say, Sarah, is that I'm going to have this baby—and I'm terribly afraid because I don't have a single close friend to be with me. I know it is awful to ask this, but is there *any* way that you could come and stay with me at least until the baby comes? I have the money to send you for your fare, and it would mean so much to have my best friend here during this hard time. Please try to come. I'm depending on you.

Sarah put down the letter and frowned. She had been apprehensive about her friend's marriage, for Abigail had indeed been spoiled. Sarah had liked Albert at once, but he was very young and apparently had very little money.

She got up and walked through the house aimlessly. She sat for a while beside Morena, smoothing her sister's blonde hair and helping with the game she was playing. Morena was ten physically, but would never be more than two or three years old mentally. She was a sweet, very beautiful girl and won the hearts of all who saw her.

As Sarah guided the youngster's hands in a simple game that involved a stick and a ball, she tried to imagine what it would be like to be in a strange place with none of your own family and be expecting a first baby. And even as she sat there, she made up her mind.

I'll have to go to be with Abigail. Somehow I just have to!

Sarah said nothing to anyone until late that night. Just when her mother was getting ready to go to bed, Sarah stopped her. "I want to talk to you, Ma."

"What is it, Sarah?"

Sarah took Abigail's letter from her pocket and handed it to her mother.

Mrs. Carter read it quickly and looked up. "You want to go to her, don't you?"

"I have to, Ma. She's the best friend I've ever had—and she's so alone and so frightened. Will it be all right?"

"It will be all right with me." Then a thought seemed to come to her, and she said, "One thing troubles me. They say that the Confederate army might be planning to invade the North again. Do you suppose they would get as far as Pennsylvania?"

"Oh, I don't think so," Sarah answered quickly. "But in any case, I'll have to go."

Mrs. Carter had the same blonde hair and green eyes as Leah. She was a warm-hearted, strong woman, and now she made an instant decision. "Your father may worry about you, as I will—but I think it's the right thing for you to do."

Two weeks after that conversation, Sarah settled into her seat and looked out the open window of the wood-burning train. Her father was on the platform, and her mother, and Leah, who was holding Morena's hand. They all waved furiously, and as the train picked up speed, she called out, "Don't worry about me! I'll be all right!"

She could not hear their answer as the train left the small town station, but she waved until they disappeared from sight. Then she listened for a while to the clicking of the steel wheels over the tracks and felt a touch of fear. It was a long way to Pennsylvania, and she had never gone anywhere by herself—not this far at least. But then she thought, *I'm nineteen years old, and God will take care of me!*

These two facts reassured her, and Sarah Carter leaned back and watched the trees rush by as the train moved steadily north.

2

The Rebels
Are Coming!

When Sarah looked out the train window at the
Gettysburg station, she saw no sign of Abigail. The
trip had been long and arduous, and her back was
stiff as she rose and gathered up her two suitcases.

A tall, lanky sergeant wearing a blue uniform
stepped up, saying, "Here, lemme take that for you,
miss."

"Why, thank you, Sergeant." Sarah had been
besieged constantly by younger members of the
Union army on board the train. At first they had
been shy, but during the long journey more than
one of them had artfully managed to sit beside her
and strike up a conversation.

Sarah noted that the sergeant wore a wedding
ring. "You're a long way from your family,
Sergeant."

"Yes, ma'am, I am. They're all the way back in
Indiana—but they're doing well, last report." The
sergeant picked up her two bags in his hamlike
hands and simply plowed his way through the pri-
vates who had clustered in the aisle. "Make way
there, you jaybirds! Give a lady room."

The sergeant stepped off the train, put down
the bags, then reached back and helped Sarah to
the platform.

"Thank you so much, Sergeant," she said. "I pray that the Lord will be with you in the days to come."

"Why, that's right kind of you, miss," the sergeant said, his eyes opening wide. "I'll appreciate your prayers."

Sarah smiled and began to search the crowd that had met the train. Actually, no more than twenty or thirty people were there, and none of them, she saw at once, looked anything like Abigail Munson.

I suppose she's getting too close to her time to be meeting trains, Sarah thought. She walked toward the small building that served as an office, but before she could step inside she was intercepted by a feminine voice.

"Miss Carter? Sarah Carter?"

Sarah turned to see a young woman coming toward her. "Why, yes, I'm Sarah Carter."

The girl was no older than nineteen. She was of medium height and had bright blue eyes and light hair. "I'm so glad to find you," she said. "My name's Jenny Wade. I'm a friend of Abigail's. She asked me to meet you."

"Is she all right?"

"Oh, yes, she's fine. Just not getting around too much right now. I've got a carriage. Where are your bags?"

Jenny Wade at once took over, and soon the two girls were in a small buggy pulled by a single gray mare.

"Get up there, Helen!" Jenny Wade said, slapping the reins on the animal's back. "That's a funny name for a horse, isn't it? Helen. I named her after a doll I had that got burned up when I was a little girl."

"We have a horse on our farm back in Kentucky named Gertrude." Sarah smiled. "I didn't name her, but I always thought it was a nice name." She looked around the streets as they passed along. "How many people are in Gettysburg?"

Jenny shrugged her shoulders. "I don't know, really. I suppose nearly a thousand if you count everyone close by. There's some students out at the seminary, but most of the young men are gone to the war."

"How is Abigail doing, Miss Wade?"

"Oh, call me Jenny." The girl smiled prettily. "She's not really doing as well as we'd like. The doctor says she might have a difficult time."

The two girls talked about Abigail and the baby that was to come until finally they turned onto a side street lined with white frame houses, most with oak trees in the yard.

Jenny suddenly asked, "Have you got a sweetheart, Sarah?"

Sarah flushed at the question but then managed a smile. "Well, not really, Jenny. Have you?"

"Oh, yes, I have—a soldier. I'm engaged to Johnston Skelly. Isn't that a funny name? I'll be Mrs. Jenny Skelly. And Johnston—that's a last name I always tell him. But that's what they called him."

"When do you plan to get married?"

"Soon. As soon as he gets back. He's due to get a leave—I think within the next three months sometime."

"You mean you'll marry him before he goes back to the army?"

"Oh, yes. Johnston argued with me, but I always could twist him around my little finger. He's so sweet, and I'm so mean to him that sometimes I'm downright ashamed of myself!"

Sarah could not imagine this cheerful young woman being mean to anyone, and she listened as Jenny spoke of her fiancé. Finally Jenny pulled up in front of one of a line of buildings on a fairly busy street.

"Abigail lives upstairs over that shop there. See the windows?"

Looking up, Sarah saw a sign that said MATTHEW'S GUN SHOP. A set of stairs opened up beside the shop, and farther up she saw curtained windows on the second floor.

She stepped out of the carriage, and Jenny tied the mare to the hitching rail.

"We can carry your bags up. You take this one." Jenny led the way to the stairs, and they ascended a set of rather steep, narrow steps. There was no light except from the doorway below, and Sarah climbed carefully.

Arriving at the landing at the top, Jenny knocked on the door. "Abigail? It's us. We're here!"

There was a long pause, and then the door opened slowly. Light from a window blotted out all except the figure that stood there. Then Sarah heard Abigail's voice calling her name. She stepped forward and was grabbed at once in a close embrace.

"Oh, Sarah. I'm so glad you're here!"

Sarah hugged the young woman and then stepped to one side so that Jenny could enter carrying a bag. "I'm glad to be here, Abigail," she said. "It was so nice of you to ask me." She put it like this so that there would be no feeling of obligation or debt in Abigail's mind.

Jenny disappeared into a side room, then came back. "I put her bags in the spare bedroom. I'll let you two talk now, but you're coming over to have supper with us tonight. Come about five o'clock."

"You can tell me more about Johnston then," Sarah teased. "And I'll bet you even have some pictures of him you want me to see."

Jenny laughed. "Yes, I do. Lots of 'em. I'll see you at supper time."

When she disappeared, Abigail said, "Come and sit down. You must be tired from that long trip."

"Actually, I'm more tired of sitting than anything else," Sarah answered ruefully. But she allowed herself to be led over to a horsehide sofa beneath the window that looked out on the street and sat down beside Abigail.

Now she had a chance to look at her friend closely and saw that the young woman's face was pale and lined with strain. However, she thought, *I'll feed you up and get you to feeling better now that I'm here.* Abigail was a very small girl with brown hair and brown eyes. She had always been pretty but rather timid, and she had surprised everyone by leaving her hometown to marry a Northerner.

"Now," Sarah said, "tell me everything."

Abigail's narration was woven with the events that had happened since she left Kentucky. She seemed to be anxious to talk, as if she had had no one to talk with, and she spoke a great deal of Albert, her husband, who was in the Union army serving under General Grant.

25

Finally Abigail drew a deep breath and laughed shortly with some embarrassment. "I'm going to talk your ear off," she said. "Why don't we fix some hot chocolate? You always loved that, didn't you, Sarah?"

"I still do. But you sit and watch me fix it. I've come to take care of you, and I might as well learn where everything is."

The girls crossed to the part of the large room that served as a kitchen. Actually the apartment consisted of one large room—a combination kitchen, dining room, and living area—plus two smaller rooms, which served as bedrooms.

As Sarah prepared the hot chocolate, heating water on a small woodstove, she thought, *It's a good thing I came. Abigail always was a little afraid of things—and she doesn't look as well as I'd like.* However, when she poured the hot chocolate into cups, she let none of this show in her face. "Now," she said, "let me tell you what's been happening back in Pineville."

As the days passed, Sarah was even more satisfied that she had done the right thing in coming to help her friend. Abigail's husband had only an uncle and aunt, who lived seven miles out in the country, and his widowed mother, who kept an apartment downtown. She was not in good health and was able to do very little for Abigail. Abigail, of course, was almost frantic with relief at having someone to be with her. She missed her own mother and family, and she threw herself into Sarah's care.

Sarah soon discovered that Jenny Wade was closer to Abigail than anyone else. Jenny was in the apartment almost every day, bringing food, helping, making clothes for the baby, and, of course, talking constantly about Johnston Skelly.

She brought all his letters. The young man was a prolific writer. He wrote about his activities as a soldier, and Jenny would carefully skip over some parts, her face blushing.

"Those are the parts I really want to hear," Sarah teased. Jenny giggled. "You'll have to get you a sweetheart and get your own love letters." Later she relented and read aloud some of the more intimate parts of his letters. They were rather sweet, and the young man was very lonely and longed to be back with his Jenny.

Every day Sarah walked the streets of Gettysburg. The talk, of course, was all of the war. Everyone agreed that the Confederate army was not going to give up without a terrible struggle.

"I tell you, they're headed this way," Mr. T. J. Thomas, the butcher, declared firmly. A group of people had gathered in his shop, and Thomas was chopping meat with hard strokes, punctuating his sentences. "We're not going to get by as easy as we have. I know Robert E. Lee. He's a fighter if ever there was one. First thing you know, the Army of Virginia's gonna be headed this way."

"What would you do if they did, T.J.?" an older man named Burns asked. He had a look of hard wear about him. His lips were tightly clenched.

T.J. Thomas said, "Why, I'd get me a musket and fight 'em, that's what I'd do!"

"I doubt if you even got a musket," Burns said and smiled slightly, "but that's exactly what I'd do!"

"Do you really think they'll be coming this way, Mr. Thomas?" Sarah asked nervously.

"Ain't no doubt in my mind. They're runnin' out of food down there in the South—so everybody says—and Robert E. Lee is gonna bring that Army of Northern Virginia north to feed his men. And then—look out!"

Sarah said nothing. She bought her pork chops and went home.

Later on, Jenny came over for supper, and the three girls talked—mostly about Johnston Skelly and about Albert Munson. Sarah knew Abigail and Jenny were fearful for their men, though they tried not to show it.

Finally Abigail said, "What about Tom, Sarah? You still in love with him?"

Jenny Wade perked up at once, her blue eyes sparkling. "Oh? So you *do* have a sweetheart, Sarah! I thought you might. No girl as pretty as you could get by without being courted."

"Oh, well—" Sarah shrugged "—we were court- ing, but he left Kentucky and joined the Confederate army. He and his whole family moved to Virginia."

"Oh, that's too bad!" Jenny exclaimed, her tone sympathetic. "That must be very hard on you."

"Yes," Abigail put in, "especially since your own brother's in the Union army. Wouldn't it be awful if they met each other on the field of battle?"

Distress came over Sarah, for she had thought exactly of this possibility. That had been the reason she could not agree to marry Tom Majors. "I try not to think about it," she said finally.

Abigail and Jenny exchanged glances, and then Abigail said quickly, "Well, when the war is over, I expect you and Tom can get together."

"What do you think will happen if the Rebels come this way?" Jenny asked.

"Oh, they'll never get this far north," Abigail said firmly. "There's not enough of them, and General Grant would never let that happen."

Then she turned the talk to babies, and Sarah felt relief to talk of something other than the war.

3

Lee Moves North

Jeff Majors stared at the food on his tin plate and shook his head mournfully. "I sure hope they don't have goober peas in heaven," he muttered. "I think I've eaten enough of 'em down here on earth."

"Why, Jeff, you ought to be glad to get good cookin' like that." The speaker was an undersized boy of fourteen with tow-colored hair and blue eyes. Charlie Bowers had been with Jeff since the two had enlisted as drummer boys, and now he winked around at the rest of the squad, who were consuming their rations.

"I don't think Jeff appreciates our cook, Curley. Why don't you explain to him how lucky he is to have you?"

Curley Henson was a huge red-haired man. It was his turn to serve as cook for the squad, and he grunted, "If he don't like the way I cook goober peas, he can cook 'em himself." He looked over at Jeff. "If you'd get out and find me something to cook—like maybe a good suckling pig—I'd show you something!"

Jeff Majors knew he was on dangerous ground. In the Confederate Army the rations were doled out, and every squad did its own cooking, the men usually taking turns at the task. Jed Hawkins was the best cook, but he had been wounded and was recuperating in the hospital.

"I wasn't complaining about the cooking, Curley," Jeff said. "I don't think there *is* any way to cook goober peas that'd make me like 'em anymore."

"Well, I expect we'll be on the march soon. We'll get better grub then." Sergeant Henry Mapes was a rangy man with black eyes and dark hair. He had been a sergeant in Jeff's company ever since Jeff had enlisted. Now he chewed thoughtfully on a piece of hardtack. "That'd be one good thing about headin' out. Those Yankees got good farms up there."

Jeff shook his head. "I doubt if General Lee'd let us help ourselves. You know how he is about things like that." Jeff was sixteen but could have passed for eighteen. He had the blackest hair possible. He was tall for his age and had grown so rapidly during the past months that the shirt he wore was too small for him. He looked over toward where the officers were having a meeting and said, "I'd like to hear what they're saying."

"Well, you can ask your pa." Sergeant Mapes grinned. "That's one good thing about having an officer for your pa. He'll always give you the information about what the army's gonna do."

"Well, shoot, *I* know what we're gonna do." Pete Simmons, a tall, very thin young man with rusty hair and blue eyes, finished his peas and hardtack, then took a swallow of water from his canteen. "We're gonna go whip the Yankees. That's what I come to do." Simmons was a new recruit. He had not been through the earlier battles and was eager to fight. The other soldiers, who had been through hard fighting since Bull Run, were sometimes amused but sometimes irritated by Pete Simmons.

31

"Wait'll you hear a few minié balls whiz around your ears," Curley Henson said in disgust. "Then we'll see how anxious you are."

Pete shook his head stubbornly. "Everybody knows one Rebel can whip five of them blue-belly Yankees."

This was a popular saying at the beginning of the war, but the members of the Stonewall Brigade had discovered it was not very close to the truth.

Jeff spoke up, saying, "You'll change your mind about that. Some of those fellows are the fightingest folks I ever saw."

"Well, I ain't no drummer boy—I'm a soldier," Pete said. It was true that he was the best shot in the entire company, and he seemed to be totally fearless, but training was one thing, and an actual battle was something else. Pete was a wild young man who drank a great deal whenever he could get whiskey and boasted about his conquests among young women. He never shirked his duty, however, and for that reason was a welcome addition to the squad.

We've lost so many men, Jeff was thinking, and a series of faces rose in his memory as he recalled those who had been in the company at the beginning of the war. Face after face came to him, all of them youthful, some of them now buried on the fields of Antietam and Fredericksburg and Bull Run. Others had been maimed beyond further fighting, and as Jeff looked around he saw that the ranks indeed were thin.

"Well, you try to find out from Captain Majors which way we're gonna go," Sergeant Mapes said.

Even as he spoke, Jeff saw his brother, Tom, approaching. Tom was a sergeant now and had the same tall, dark good looks as their father. Jeff called out, "Well, what's the word, brother?"

Tom Majors sat down and took a pan of peas and some hardtack and began to eat hungrily. "Well, General Lee didn't tell me all of his plans—" he grinned, his white teeth flashing "—but I expect everybody knows we're not gonna sit around here much longer."

Soon a card game began. Jeff had discovered that soldiering was rather odd. Either it was as boring as anything he'd ever done—for weeks doing absolutely nothing except light drill—or for brief moments it was filled with absolute terror as the shells and bullets passed through the ranks and men died.

Jeff pulled Tom to one side and reached into his pocket. "A letter came for you from Pineville."

Tom's dark eyes brightened. He took the letter and started off.

"Aren't you going to read it to me?" Jeff protested. Then he grinned as Tom merely shook his head and walked away. "Must be awful to be in love like that," he muttered to himself. He knew that a letter from Sarah Carter was the biggest event in his brother's life. The two had been practically engaged before the war, and even now he knew Tom wanted to marry Sarah more than he wanted anything else in the world.

Thinking of Sarah brought memories of the times before the war when Leah, Sarah's younger sister, had been the biggest thing in his own life. Jeff leaned back and half closed his eyes, listening to the talk flow over him.

He was so accustomed to camp sounds that he barely heard a bugle blowing and the shouts of command or saw the cavalry that rode by at almost full speed, raising dust. He was thinking instead of Leah and how they had searched for birds' eggs and fished in the creeks of Kentucky and hunted possum and coon at night.

Leah's face came before him. She was fifteen now, he knew, but somehow he still thought of her as younger than that. He remembered with a guilty feeling that he owed her a letter, and he stirred himself finally to find paper and a pencil and soon was busily filling the sheet with a record of his activities.

Capt. Nelson Majors was perhaps the finest-looking officer in the Stonewall Brigade. He was six feet tall and weighed 175 pounds. His skin was dark. He had black hair and hazel eyes. Recently he had cultivated a mustache, which made him look very dashing. He wore his gray uniform with grace, for he had always been a man who could make clothes look good no matter how simple they were.

Coming out of the colonel's tent, Majors wandered through the camp, his sharp black eyes taking in everything. He had just been told that his promotion had come through. But promotion meant little to him. His only concern was his company. He would do no more with the new rank of major than he had done with the rank of captain.

He found his way to where Jeff and Tom were sitting out in front of their tents and smiled as they rose. He was intensely proud of these young men and noted that Jeff was almost as tall as Tom now, although not as heavy. Both looked a great deal like him, and he regretted wishing that one of them looked like their mother. But he was encouraged to think that his daughter, Esther, still only a baby, looked very much like his late wife.

He still missed his wife terribly and longed to see his child. She was, however, in Kentucky being cared for by the Carter family until after the war. He thought warmly of Dan and Mary Carter and once again thought, *There are no finer people in the world than those two!*

Drawing up in front of his sons, he said, "You're invited to have supper with one of your officers tonight." He grinned then, saying, "I've got a surprise for you. I've been promoted."

Tom grinned happily back. "I wondered how long it would be before they recognized how badly they needed you, Pa—I mean Major."

"Now you'll be Major Majors, won't you? That's an odd thing," Jeff put in.

Nelson Majors took his boys to a café in the main part of Richmond. He ordered the best they had in the house, which in this case was steak and potatoes, and the three ate hungrily.

Tom grinned at his father and winked, nodding toward Jeff. "Look at him lay his ears back and fly at it. I've never seen such a hog!"

"You're not doing too bad yourself, Tom," Jeff managed to say around a mouthful of hot potatoes. He cut a chunk off his T-bone steak, his eyes dreamy with pleasure.

Major Majors looked at his sons and felt again both pride and fear. He was proud of their accomplishments. They were good soldiers, both of them. Tom at twenty and Jeff at only sixteen were as good as any soldiers in the regiment. Maybe in the whole army as far as he was concerned. But he had seen too many like these two lying dead on the field of battle. He did not fear for himself, but he was troubled about them and about what would happen to Esther should he lose his life. He had not spoken of this to Tom or Jeff for there was nothing to be done. The three were soldiers and had to fight, but it was never far from his mind.

They finished off their meal with peach pie and imitation coffee, which made them all frown.

"They must make this out of pecan shells," Tom muttered. "It sure doesn't taste much like coffee, does it?"

"Maybe some'll come in on one of the blockade runners," the major replied.

They were talking of the battle that was to come when suddenly Tom said, "You know, Pa—I mean Major," he amended hastily, "I've been thinking. What would happen to Esther if we weren't able to take care of her?"

Looking up quickly, Nelson Majors understood that Tom had been thinking exactly as he had. "Well," he said, "if something happened to me, you boys would have to take over."

Jeff said, "Yes, but what if something happens to us too? Don't like to think about it, but it could happen."

"Esther's in good hands," Nelson said slowly. "The Carters have been so good to take her. If something did happen, they would raise her in a Christian way." He did not want to talk about this and said instead, "She's doing fine. I miss her a great deal though. Not right for a girl child not to have her father and family around."

Jeff had spent more time than the other two at the Carter house. He had made more than one visit back there. "You wouldn't ever know her name's not

36

Esther Carter. They baby her to death. She'll be spoiled rotten, Pa—I mean Major."

"I know, but I wish *we* could do those things for her—spoil her, that is."

"We will when it's all over." Tom nodded firmly. "One of these days this war'll be over, and we can get Esther and get us a farm, and it'll be great."

"It's not just Esther you're thinking about, though," Jeff said slyly. He saw Tom give him a warning look and said only, "Don't shoot! I guess we'd all like to see Sarah and Leah and all the folks there again."

The three finished their pie and walked back toward camp. There was more movement than usual.

"I expect we'll be pulling out of here pretty soon," the major said.

He was right about that, for the next morning bugles were blowing and officers were meeting. Everyone in the army knew that great things were afoot.

Late that afternoon Jeff got the word from Tom, who had gotten it from his father. "We'll be pulling out. You got anything to do, you'd better do it."

Jeff, along with the rest of the squad, began making hasty preparations. None of them knew how long they would be gone. All of them were certain they would be moving north to attack the Yankees on their own ground. This had happened once before, but they had been stopped at Antietam. Now, however, the Army of Northern Virginia was fit and ready and well-equipped, better than it had ever been.

It took two days to get the army ready to roll, and when they were about to leave, the streets of Richmond were lined with people gathered to see them off.

Jeff and Charlie Bowers stood in place with their drums as a band began to play. The troops paraded through the crowded streets with flags flying and banners waving, and there was a thrill in Jeff's heart as he thought, *I'm a part of all this. Next year I'll be old enough to be a regular soldier. But even now I'm part of it.*

The company was dismissed after the parade, and there was a time of farewells for the soldiers who had families present.

Jeff was standing to one side watching all this when he heard his name called. He turned to see Lucy Driscoll coming toward him.

Lucy was a small, well-shaped girl of fourteen. Her blonde hair was tied back, and her blue eyes were bright. She wore a white dress with blue trim on the collar and sleeves that matched her eyes. She stopped exactly in front of him. "Oh, Jeff! I thought I'd missed you!" she cried.

Jeff smiled down at her. He remembered that the first time he had met Lucy he hadn't had to look down so far. There had been times when she had not been his favorite, but their friendship had survived, and now he said simply, "Nice of you to come out and tell us good-bye."

Lucy made a fetching picture as she looked up at him, but her face was troubled. "I'm proud of you, Jeff—but I'm worried too."

"Why, don't worry, Lucy," he said airily. "We'll go up and whip the Yankees and then come back, and it'll all be over."

But his light remarks obviously did not convince Lucy. She shook her head, and Jeff was astonished to see sudden tears in her eyes.

"Please be careful," she said. "I don't want anything to happen to you."

Jeff stared at her, unable to speak for a moment.

Then suddenly, to his shock and amazement, Lucy threw her arms around him and kissed him soundly, right on the lips!

"There!" she said defiantly and then laughed. "I'm getting to be downright bold, aren't I?"

Jeff could still feel the pressure of her soft lips. He could not think of a single intelligent thing to say. "Ahhh—why, Lucy!" he exclaimed.

But then she turned and fled, calling back, "Don't forget me." Jeff stood there dumbfounded. He had not known Lucy cared that much for him.

"Well, now, it's nice to have a sweetheart come and kiss you good-bye, ain't it now?"

An elbow struck Jeff in the side, and he turned to see Pete Simmons grinning at him.

"I didn't know you was such a ladies' man, Jeff," he said. "Who was that pretty little thing?"

Jeff did not want to talk about Lucy to Pete Simmons, and he said, "Oh, just a friend."

"Looked like a pretty good friend to me." Pete laughed. "When we get back here, you'll have to introduce me to her."

At that moment the bugles sounded, and Jeff hurried back to his position. The company formed, and he began to rattle out with the drum, Charlie Bowers beside him, grinning. Then the army started to move, making a long, serpentine column as they curved through the streets of Richmond.

39

Finally they were outside the city, and Jeff looked forward, still wondering what lay ahead of them up North. He remembered other young men who had started out like this and who had never returned, and now the thought of how uncertain life was came to him.

4
"God Is Always There"

The Confederate Army that moved out of Virginia, crossed the Potomac, and advanced into Pennsylvania shocked the Northern farmers. They had been accustomed to the neat blue uniforms, the spotless muskets, and other fine equipment of the Federal troops. When the Army of Northern Virginia passed into their territory, some of the militia men took one look at Jubal Early's veterans and took to their heels at once.

Gettysburg civilians never forgot their sight of the famed foot soldiers of Gen. Robert E. Lee. "Most of the men," recalled one farmer, "were exceedingly dirty, some ragged, some without shoes, and some surrounded by skeletons of what had once been an entire hat." However, he noted, they were all armed and under perfect discipline, adding, "They seemed to move like one vast machine."

On the other hand, Jeff was amazed at the wealth of the Pennsylvania towns his unit passed through. To eyes accustomed to the countryside of Virginia, stripped by the ravages of war, these rolling fields, huge farms, and prosperous towns seemed almost a miracle.

"Looks like we could just move in here, doesn't it, Tom?" he muttered as they marched into York and noted its prosperity.

It was a rare scene—invading army and invaded population hobnobbing on the public green.

Many Southern sympathizers were there. But some of them had gotten together a band that struck up "Yankee Doodle" as the Confederates marched into town.

The general made a rattling speech, saying among other things, "My friends, how do you like our way of coming back into the Union? I hope you like it, for I have been in favor of it a long time. We're not burning your houses or butchering your children. On the contrary, we are behaving ourselves like Christian gentlemen, which we are."

"Sounds like he's running for office, don't he?" Pete Simmons said to Jeff. "I guess politicians all sound the same, North or South."

They paused that night, rested, and left the next day with their supply wagons filled.

Not all Pennsylvania towns were as receptive to the invasion as York, however. In Harrisburg everything was bedlam. The railroad station was crowded with trunks, boxes, bundles, and packages. Mobs rushed here and there in a frantic manner, shouting, screaming as if the Rebels were about to dash into town and lay it in ashes. The railroads were removing their cars and engines. The merchants were packing up their goods. Housewives were secreting their silver, and everywhere there was a scene of mad excitement and despair.

At noon the following day, Jeff and his company were marching along the dusty road through a little town called Greencastle. There was almost a holiday air about the march. Soldiers shouted at one another and sang marching songs, and as they passed through the small town the band played "Dixie."

They were just going by a vine-covered house when a young girl no more than twelve rushed out onto the front porch. She was waving, Jeff saw, a United States flag. He was almost even with the house when she cried out, "Traitors! Traitors! Come and take this flag, the man of you who dares!"

Gen. George Pickett happened to be riding past at the time. He pulled his coal black stallion to a halt and took off his hat. He bowed to the girl and saluted her flag, then turned to look at the troops. Jeff and every other man in sight of the girl raised his cap and cheered her till the air rang with the noise of their voices.

The girl was taken aback. She lowered her flag and stared at the ragged soldiers in front of her. Finally, tears came into her eyes, and she called out, "Oh, I wish I had a Rebel flag. I'd wave that too!"

The unit marched all day, and that night Jeff's squad feasted. General Lee had put out an order that no food was to be stolen or taken by force from the citizens, but somehow Pete Simmons had managed to "liberate" a young pig. He brought it back, and, despite a stern lecture from Sergeant Henry Mapes, the pig had been butchered, and soon the air was filled with the delicious smell of fresh pork cooking. Other soldiers had purchased fresh buttermilk from some local farmers and freshly baked bread from one of the bakeries in the small town.

The squad sat around eating, and afterward Jeff leaned back and listened to a group of soldiers singing down the line. They sang a familiar ballad called "Tenting Tonight on the Old Campground." It was one of the most popular songs on both sides. Its appeal was so strong that officers had to restrain their men from singing it at night because they would give away their positions on the field. Sleepy and tired, Jeff listened to the words floating over the landscape.

After the voices of the singers died down, Tom began to talk of what lay ahead. "Sooner or later we're gonna run into more blue-bellies than any of us ever saw," he said quietly. He seemed moody, poking the fire with a stick, and Jeff knew he was thinking of Sarah Carter.

Pete Simmons had no worries, however. He laughed and slapped Tom on the shoulder. "You just wait, Tom," he said. "We'll give 'em fits this time."

Jed Hawkins, small, lean, and with his sharp features looking more like a fox than anything else, shook his head. "Some of us won't be coming back from this trip," he murmured.

"That's right. Don't do no harm to think of that," Charlie said. He was the smallest of the group—and perhaps the most fervent Christian. He had been converted in a camp meeting, led to the Lord by no less than Gen. Stonewall Jackson. He looked around and said, "Hope all you fellers are ready to meet the Lord."

Most of the men in the squad were Christians, but Pete Simmons kicked at the ground in disgust, raising a puff of dust. "I don't want to hear no sermons," he said grumpily. "I hear enough out of that chaplain that keeps nagging at me."

Chaplain Finias Rawlings was indeed a man to keep after his flock. Jeff had heard him try to talk to Pete only two days prior. Pete had simply told the chaplain to go find somebody else to do his preaching to.

That bothered Jeff, for he liked Pete. Now he said, "Better listen to him, Pete. He's telling you the

44

truth. Even if there wasn't any war, I'd rather be a Christian than not."

Pete leaned over and ruffled Jeff's hair. "Listen to me, drummer boy," he said, "I'll think about things like that when I'm too old to chase after the girls and do my drinking."

"May not have time for that," Sgt. Henry Mapes said. He stretched his long, rangy body and looked northward.

It was the thirtieth of June, and the night was hot. The army had pulled up for a rest while the scouts went out.

Mapes shook his head dolefully. "I got a bad feeling about this fight. It's gonna be worse than usual."

The next day they moved again. This time it was Jeff who decided to go out and see if he could find more food for the unit. He obtained his lieutenant's permission and found himself walking along a country road lined on either side by huge fields. A few times he saw men out working in them.

He decided to turn in at a prosperous-looking farmhouse. He felt a little apprehensive, for he was not sure how people would feel about a Confederate soldier. There had been occasions when some of their number had been shot at by the civilian enemy from cover.

Keeping a sharp eye out, he stepped up on the porch of the well-cared-for house and knocked.

The door opened almost at once, and a short, rather heavy woman stood in front of him. "What does thee want?"

Something about her speech made Jeff hesitate for a moment. "Well, ma'am," he said, "what I'd

45

really like to do is buy some food if you'd sell it to me."

"Is thee one of the Confederates?"

Again Jeff wondered briefly at her use of "thee" instead of "you."

"Yes, I am. I'm a member of the Stonewall Brigade, ma'am."

The woman stepped outside and looked at Jeff more closely. She had a cheerful, round red face. Her eyes were gray, and she had an abundant head of attractive auburn hair. Jeff thought she was pretty. She was wearing a plain gray dress and no jewelry whatsoever. She studied him in a most peculiar way as if he were an exhibit in a zoo.

Jeff grew nervous and finally blurted out, "I don't want to steal anything. We don't do that in our army."

"Come inside, young man."

Jeff was surprised. However, he followed her into the house, noting that it too was very plain without a great deal of ornamentation. The furniture was pretty though. He'd never seen any exactly like it before. Pictures and paintings and tintypes hung on the walls, and he saw that all the people in them were wearing plain dark clothes. *A rather stern-looking bunch,* he thought.

"We have a visitor."

The woman spoke to the man who was coming into the kitchen through another door. Jeff saw that he was small and as lean as his wife was fat. He had a shock of thick salt-and-pepper hair and mild brown eyes. "What hast thee found, Ellie? A soldier boy?"

"Yes, sir," Jeff spoke up quickly. "I'm in General Lee's army. I stopped to see if I could buy some food."

"What is thy name, young man?"

"Jeff Majors."

"My name is Claude Poteet, and this is my wife, Ellie." He was carrying a bucket of fresh milk, and he set it down on the counter. "Wife, we'll have some fresh milk and perhaps some of that apricot cake that thee made yesterday."

Jeff's mouth watered at the thought of apricot cake, and soon he found himself sitting at a plain pine table, trying not to wolf down the cake as he would have liked to. He answered questions as best he could with his mouth full, and he thought he'd never tasted anything as good as the warm fresh milk.

Claude Poteet asked many questions about Jeff and about the army and soon said, "Is thee a God-fearing young man, Jeff?"

"Well—" Jeff swallowed a mouthful of milk and wiped his mouth with his sleeve "—I'm a Christian, Mr. Poteet."

"I'm glad to hear it." Poteet nodded. "We are Friends here."

"Friends?"

"Thee would call us Quakers."

"Oh, I know about Quakers," Jeff said instantly, remembering. "I met one not long ago that did me a great favor—took care of me when I was hurt."

"Well, we Friends don't believe in violence, so we don't fight in the war, but we take care of the wounded when we can," Ellie Poteet put in. "Try another piece of this cake."

47

Jeff sat there feeling quite at home, and within a short time the Poteets heard his life history.

Then Ellie Poteet, after a look at her husband, said, "Does thee feel we might have this young man's father and brother for supper, husband?"

"That would be well if it could be done."

"Oh, our unit's not far down the road. My father's the major, and my brother's a sergeant. They'd be glad to come."

"Good. As soon as thee finishes thy cake, go get them. I'll go kill one of our fattest fowls for supper tonight."

Supper at the Poteets' was a success. Jeff guessed that his father was far more handsome and cultured than the couple had expected, and they were impressed with his manners and with his bearing.

Ellie Poteet said, "Thee can never deny that these are thy boys. The family resemblance is strong. Does thee have other children, Major?"

"One girl, just a baby. Her name is Esther." He hesitated, then said sadly, "I lost my wife when she was born."

"Well, the Lord comfort thee," Claude Poteet said with compassion in his voice. "We have lost two of our own, so we know the pain."

The meal was the best any of them had had for months—fried chicken, fresh ham, and such vegetables as were available, including fried squash, which was a favorite with Jeff. He ate so much of it that Ellie Poteet warned him mildly, "Thee is going to burst, young man."

Jeff grinned at her. "It'd be a wonderful way to die! Fried squash is about as good as food gets."

Afterward they adjourned to the parlor and drank real coffee. Nelson Majors had four cups of it before holding his hand up and saying, "That will have to do me. You can't drink enough to store it for the future, can you?" He looked at the Poteets and smiled. "We all appreciate your hospitality. It's been a wonderful evening, but we must get back to our unit."

"Before thee goes, we will pray for thee."

The three soldiers stood up, and the Quakers prayed with them one at a time, standing on either side. First they prayed heartily for Nelson Majors, for his safety and for his motherless daughter. Then they prayed for Tom that he would be kept safe in the battle and that he would live to see his "children's children"—Ellie's exact words. Tom stared at her when she finished, and Jeff knew he was thinking of Sarah and of getting married.

Then they came to Jeff and put their hands on his shoulders. He felt the warmth of them. One, then the other, prayed. "Lord, guide this fine young man. Let not war make him grow bitter. Keep him sweet in Thy Spirit. . ." It was quite a long prayer, and Jeff felt very good about it.

As the three soldiers walked back down the dark road to where the regiment was camped, Nelson Majors said briefly, "If everybody in the world was as kind and loving as the Poteets, it would be a good place to live!"

5
Time for a Birth

As the time for the birth of Abigail's baby grew close, Sarah grew more and more concerned. The two young women were alone for the most part—although Jenny Wade still came by frequently. They were sitting one day making sheets for the baby when the door flew open and Jenny burst in, her eyes wide with excitement.

"The Rebels are coming! They're on their way here!"

At once Abigail became flustered, her face grew pale, and she tried to struggle to her feet, crying out, "When—where—"

"Now you sit down there, Abigail." Sarah soothed her friend and eased her back into the chair. "It's all probably rumors.   There's always plenty of those. We've heard them for days now."

"It's no rumor this time," Jenny protested. Her face was flushed, and she shook her head, sending her curls swinging on the back of her neck. "Mr. Thompson saw them. He was out on the Chambersburg Pike this morning, and he said they were camped all along the road there. There must be a million of them, he said."

Sarah noted that the news distressed Abigail greatly, though she herself did not get excited. "Well, they'll probably pass right on through," she said practically. "Sit down, Jenny. We have some raisin cake left."

Jenny hesitated, then shrugged and sat at the table. As Sarah made tea and cut a slice of cake for her, she continued to speak of the enormous army of Rebels that appeared to be descending upon them.

"If there're that many Confederates," Sarah said, putting the cake down in front of Jenny, "then the Union Army has to be close. I've been reading in the paper that General Hooker has been following the Confederate troops all the way from Richmond."

"Well, where *are* they?" Abigail asked, her voice tense. "Oh, why did it have to come at a time like this?" She began to cry, and her friends both went around to pat her shoulders and comfort her.

"There, there, Abigail," Jenny said. "Dr. Morse will be right here, and you won't have any trouble."

"Oh, I will! I just know I will!"

"You'll be fine," Sarah said encouragingly. She patted Abigail's hand, then held it. "I'll be right here, and Jenny—and Dr. Morse is a fine doctor."

Sarah and Jenny stayed beside Abigail until she grew calm, then resumed their seats.

When Jenny bit into the raisin cake, she exclaimed, "Oh, this is good! I wish Johnston had some of this. It was always one of his favorites."

"Have you heard from him lately?" Sarah inquired.

"Yes, I got a letter just this morning. I brought it with me. I'll read you part of it."

Sarah and Abigail listened as Jenny read, and Sarah was pleased at the excitement on the young woman's face. Johnston Skelly proclaimed his love as he always did by saying,

51

I'd hoped to be able to come home on leave, but it seems I'll be sent with other troops under General Grant to Tennessee. It shouldn't take too long to run the Rebels out of there, sweetheart, and then I'll be coming home, and we'll be married. Can't wait for that day to come.

With all my love,
Your soldier boy,
Johnston Skelly

"I know you're disappointed," Sarah remarked. "You were counting on his coming home."

"Oh, yes, I was. I've got my wedding dress all made and a whole chest full of linens . . ." Jenny's face grew sad. "Sometimes I think it'll never be over, this awful war."

Sarah had thought the same thing many times, but this was no time to add to the gloom. As cheerfully as she could, she said, "Well, it will be. All things come to an end, and this war will too. Then you'll have Johnston back, and you'll have the best wedding any girl in Gettysburg ever had." She continued to speak cheerfully, and by the time Jenny went home even Abigail seemed to have lost her fears.

Sarah read to Abigail for some time, but the expectant mother's attention appeared to wander. She was in considerable discomfort, Sarah noticed, and nothing she could do seemed to ease it. Finally she closed the book. "I think it's time for you to go to bed. You've had a hard day."

"All right." Abigail sighed. She got to her feet slowly and moved into her bedroom.

Sarah saw to it that she got to bed. Then she leaned over and kissed her, whispering, "It won't be long now. You'll have a fine boy—or a fine girl—and then we'll have the real joy of all of this."

Sarah went back into the living area. Taking out pencil and paper, she sat down and for more than an hour wrote letters. One was to her parents, in which she assured them that she was fine and Abigail was doing very well. She wrote also to Tom, but this letter was more difficult. Twice she got no farther than a paragraph and then tore up the sheet of paper and started over.

For a long time she sat there as darkness fell, thinking of days that were gone, thinking mostly of Tom Majors and of how they had fallen in love back in Kentucky. He had been the best-looking young man in the county, and she smiled as she thought of how other girls had tried to catch his attention. But they never had.

He always like me best, she thought, *even when we were ten years old. He carried my books to school for me—and once when Roy Abrahams called me a name, Tom jumped on him even though he was almost two years older.*

She thought of that fight and how afterward she had taken Tom to the brook and washed his bloody face with her handkerchief. Her hands had trembled, she remembered, and then she had leaned forward and kissed him—their first kiss.

The shadows fell fast outside now, and soon it was dark. She rose, lit a candle, and brought it back to the table. Finally, with a sigh, knowing that she must write something, she wrote:

Dear Tom,

I am not certain this letter will reach you. Here in Gettysburg the rumor is that the Army of Northern Virginia is headed this way. Right now you may be closer to me than we have been for many months. I wish that you were back in Virginia. My heart aches when I think of your going into battle again, but I must not trouble you with this.

She continued the letter by giving the circumstances of her visit in Gettysburg and finally ended by saying,

My dearest, I think so often of our days together when we were younger. I think of how we have been parted. It is a grief to me, but all over this country, North and South, there are other grieving young women and young men too. We must accept the will of God—but it is my prayer that one day we will be together again.

With all my affection,
Sarah Carter

She was unhappy with the letter, but anything she might write would be feeble and not express what was in her heart. She folded it, sealed it with wax, and put it aside. Then she went to bed.

Sarah lay awake for some time. Finally dropping off to sleep, she slept fitfully, tossing. The night was warm, and she threw all the covers back. Suddenly she heard a cry and awoke instantly.

In the other bedroom she found Abigail, tears on her cheeks.

54

"What is it, Abigail?" Sarah asked, going quickly to put her hand on the girl's forehead.

"I think—I think it won't be too long before the baby comes!"

Sarah hesitated, wondering if it might be the time to go for Dr. Morse. She decided, however, to wait a little while. It was nearly dawn, she saw by the mantel clock, and she said, "We'll see then, Abigail. It may be. There still should be plenty of time."

The feeble gray light touched the east, and finally the yellow sun rose. Jenny Wade came at eight o'clock.

While she and Jenny were in the outer room, Sarah said worriedly, "I'm not certain about things like this. Perhaps it would be better to go find Dr. Morse now."

"I think it might be best," Jenny agreed. "It's too bad we don't have an older woman here, but we'll just have to do the best we can."

Sarah opened her mouth to say, "I'll go—" but she broke off abruptly. "What was that?"

They stared at each other, and then it came again—a low rumble.

"That's not thunder," Jenny whispered.

No. And then Sarah knew the truth. "That's cannon fire!"

Although she had never heard a cannon fired, she knew instantly that this was the beginning of a battle. "I'd better get back to Abigail," she said.

"I'll stay with you," Jenny said.

Abigail was sitting up in bed, her face twisted with pain. "What's that noise? Is it fighting?"

"I'm afraid it is," Sarah said calmly, "but it's far off. I don't want you worrying about that. How do you feel?"

The cannon grew louder as the morning progressed, and soon Sarah heard a crackling sound.

"What's that?" Abigail started and looked fearfully toward the window.

Sarah knew it must be musket fire, and that meant the fighting was coming closer. She grew apprehensive—not for herself but for Abigail. For the next two hours she tried to soothe the frightened girl, but the firing grew louder and louder, and at the same time Abigail grew more and more terrified.

By one o'clock the battle was raging close by. Whether or not this had anything to do with Abigail's condition, neither Jenny nor Sarah was certain—but at one-thirty Sarah said, "You stay with her, Jenny. I'm going for the doctor."

Jenny went to the window and looked out. "All right, but be careful!" she said. Jenny walked out of the bedroom with Sarah, saying again, "Be careful, Sarah. I think there are enemy soldiers coming into town."

"Dr. Morse's house isn't too far. I'll get him, and we'll be right back," Sarah said.

As she went out the front door, a tremendous explosion took place somewhere to her left. Startled, she whirled to see the corner of a shop caving in. Dust and smoke filled the air, and then Sarah began to run, praying that none of the shells would hit the building where Abigail lay having her child.

I hope Dr. Morse isn't gone, she thought, breathing heavily. She wondered what she would do if he *was* gone but could do nothing more than utter a prayer that God would take care of His own.

Neither Jeff nor his companions in his squad or even in his company understood the battle that took place on July 1 at Gettysburg. It was a confusing battle to say the least.

Jeff had been roused out of a sound sleep by Lieutenant Forbes with hurried instructions. "Get on that drum, Jeff! We've got to get on the road. Everything's moving!"

Jeff rubbed the sleep out of his eyes and leaped to his feet. Then he and Charlie Bowers moved along the lines of sleeping soldiers, the sharp rattle of their drums bringing the men to their feet.

Sgt. Tom Majors appeared in the morning light, his eyes troubled. "Pa says we're going to be in a big fight. He won't be with us," he told Jeff. "You stay back when the fighting starts. You hear me?"

Jeff wanted to admonish Tom to do the same, but he knew that that would be useless. "Be careful, Tom," he said. "Don't get yourself hurt."

Tom grinned, though his dark eyes were sober. He slapped Jeff on the back, saying, "I'll be all right. Now it's time to go."

Much later, when the battle was over, Jeff went back and tried to study what had happened. Neither General Lee nor General Meade, who had taken command of the Union troops, wanted to fight at Gettysburg. Neither army was at its full strength. But the battle seemed to get out of the control of the generals.

The first action occurred in the gray light of dawn, just as the trees and fences and houses along the Chambersburg Pike began to grow clear. A group of Confederate infantrymen had approached to within a half mile of Gettysburg when they saw Federal cavalry. This cavalry was under the charge of General Buford, and Buford decided to use his men to hold the line until the full strength of the Union Army could be brought up.

The opening shots were fired, and soon both armies were engaged in a fierce skirmish. As usual, Jeff kept as close to his company as he could. At times his father was nearby, giving him commands to pass on to the fighting soldiers by means of the drum. That was the only way to give orders on the battlefield. Men could hear the drum or the bugle when they could hear nothing else above the noise of battle.

At one point, when the Union troops were charging, Jeff threw down his drum, picked up a musket from a dead Confederate, loaded it, and fired. Another time, when the fighting was at its worst, he saw Pete Simmons, his face black with powder, firing and cursing. He wished that Pete would not do that, for death was everywhere.

All morning and throughout the afternoon the battle raged. Slowly the Confederates advanced toward Gettysburg, driving the Union troops back. Then General Early delivered a smashing blow that broke the back of the Union line. The men in blue continued to fall back, and Maj. Nelson Majors shouted, "We've got 'em on the run! Charge!"

As the troops pressed forward, suddenly Charlie Bowers cried out.

Jeff was by him in a moment. "Are you hurt, Charlie?"

Charlie Bowers looked at his bleeding upper arm. "No—I mean, not bad—but I can't sound a drum with one arm!"

"You go back to where the doctors are, Charlie. I'll do the drumming!" Jeff cried. He had been terribly afraid that Charlie had been killed.

Then Jeff sprang forward, sounding his drum, as Tom led the squad. Soon they came under heavy fire from the retreating Union troops, but Tom never hesitated. "Let's go, you Rebels!" he cried, holding up his musket. With another shout he led them into the small town of Gettysburg.

6
Tom Gets a Surprise

To Tom Majors the crackle of musket fire sounded like thousands of men breaking sticks. The retreating Union soldiers were pushed back slowly, but their fire was taking a toll of the Confederates. Tom had a passion to save his squad and saw to it that they advanced carefully, taking cover behind whatever was there.

"Pete! Get down!" he yelled once, seeing Pete Simmons charging down the street, yelling and brandishing his musket.

Simmons turned, his face inflamed with battle fury. "We've got 'em on the run, Sarge. Let's get 'em!"

Musket balls zipped through the air, but Tom ran and yanked Simmons behind one of the stone buildings. "You're gonna get yourself killed!" he growled. "Then what good will you be? And is your musket loaded?"

Simmons blinked, then looked down. "No, it ain't," he said. "I just got carried away."

"Well, load it!" Tom snapped and watched as Pete expertly loaded the rifle. He thought for a moment of the breech-loading rifles some of the Federal troops had. He had heard you could load in seven shells and fire them all without reloading.

The old muskets that the Rebels carried were painstakingly hard to use. First you had to pull a paper cartridge full of powder out of your cartridge bag, bite the end of it—which left a black mark on your mouth—and pour the powder into the muzzle. After that you put a wad down there to keep the powder in place. Then you pounded a conical bullet into the barrel, after which you put in another wad to keep it from falling out. And then it was necessary to put a cap in the breech, all of which took much longer than simply inserting bullets.

The streets revealed the still bodies of blue-clad infantry, and some wounded were crawling painfully away. Tom felt grieved for the dead and wounded, but he had no time to think of them.

"Move on!" he yelled. Then, seeing Henry Mapes, he shouted, "Henry, you take that street. I'll go down this one. We'll clear them of all the Yankees."

"Right, Tom," Mapes hollered back and took a small group of the squad to angle down a side street, urging them to keep their heads down.

Tom saw no other squad members close by, so he darted into his street alone. He checked his musket to be sure that it was loaded, then advanced cautiously, his eyes darting everywhere for a sight of the enemy.

A pall of smoke had settled over Gettysburg. It had a sharp, acrid smell, but he was accustomed to that. Just then a movement caught his eye, and he whirled, throwing up his musket—but then saw it was only a large black-and-tan hound dog with floppy ears.

"Better get out of here, boy," he said shakily. "You won't be able to do any hunting if you get yourself killed."

Tom moved quickly up the street and was relieved to see none of the enemy's infantry. He had just turned the corner to angle back toward the main thoroughfare when two things happened. A woman stepped out of a doorway—and at the same moment a shell exploded over to her left.

Tom knew that it was likely the artillery would throw other shells in the same position, so he ran toward the woman at once.

He shouted at her—she was now running down the street—but the explosion of other shells drowned out his voice. He finally caught up with her, grabbed her arm, and pulled her around, yelling, "Get off the street!"

The woman turned, and Tom stared at her in astonishment. It was Sarah Carter!

Sarah was as startled as Tom looked to be. She had expected anything in the world but this—and now, as shells continued to explode and the sound of rifle fire rattled up ahead, she could not speak for a moment.

Tom dropped his musket to the ground. It clattered and could have gone off, but he paid no attention. He put his arms around her and held her close. Then he drew back and whispered hoarsely, "Sarah! What in the world—"

Sarah still stared at him. "Tom!" was all she could say.

Another shell went off down the street, and the firing sounded closer.

"What are you doing here, Sarah? You've got to get out of the street!"

"I can't, Tom. I came to help Abigail. She's having a baby, and I came to be with her."

"You can't *stay* out here!"

"But I've got to get Dr. Morse. I've got to!"

Tom looked around desperately. No blue-clad soldiers were charging up the street, but there was always that chance.

"Where's this doctor live?"

"Down the street to the left."

"Well, come on, I'll go with you." Tom snatched up his musket and, taking Sarah's arm, kept her close to the buildings.

She saw no Union soldiers, and the barrage seemed to be over momentarily.

"How long have you been here?" he asked.

When Sarah told him what was happening, Tom could only say, "Of all the people for me to find on the streets of this town, I guess you're the last one I expected."

Sarah flashed him a smile. "So good to see you, Tom. I wrote you a letter last night, but I won't have to give it to you now."

"What did you say in the letter, Sarah?"

Sarah hesitated, then stopped walking entirely and turned to him. "I said how much I thought of those days so long ago when we were children and then when we were growing up and you came courting me."

Tom looked down at her admiringly. "You were always the prettiest girl in the county," he said.

"And you were the handsomest young man."

Tom asked quietly, "What else did you say in the letter?"

"I said—" Sarah hesitated, then went on almost in a whisper "—I said that I loved you and always would. And—and I said that I'd marry you!"

And there in the middle of the Battle of Gettysburg, Tom Majors took Sarah Carter in his arms. She put her arms around his neck, pulling his head down, and he kissed her. Then he drew back and shook his head, his eyes troubled. "I've wanted to hear that more than anything in the world! But come—we can't stay here."

"Will you come back after the battle?" Sarah asked.

"I'll do the best I can."

They entered the doctor's office without knocking and found Dr. Morse inside. He was a tall, strongly built man with sparse gray hair and penetrating blue eyes.

"What's all this?" He looked at Tom with a question in his eyes.

"This is an old friend of mine from Kentucky," Sarah said. She hesitated, wondering what the doctor would think of her having friends in Confederate uniform, part of the attacking enemy. But there was no time to explain. "Dr. Morse, you've got to come! I think the baby's coming!"

At once the doctor nodded. "Been expecting it." He grabbed his black bag, pulled his hat on his head, then said, "Are you going with us, soldier?"

"I'll go with you to be sure you don't take any stray shots," Tom said.

"All right, let's go."

Sarah and the two men passed through some advancing Confederate infantry, and Tom waved them off.

"Probably just as well you're with us, young man," Dr. Morse grunted. "Hate to be taken prisoner when that woman needs me."

When they reached the doorway next to the gun shop, Sarah turned to Tom. "This is it, Tom. Come back if you can."

"I will—if I can." Tom reached out, took her hands, then suddenly kissed them. He gave the doctor a defiant look and said, "Do your best, doctor," then ran down the street toward where the firing was heaviest.

Dr. Morse was clearly curious about the situation. "I guess he's a pretty good friend of yours," he observed, his eyes taking in Sarah's face.

"Yes—yes, he is, Dr. Morse."

"Maybe more than a friend?"

"Yes, more than a friend. We were going to be married, but the war came. His family went to Virginia." Then Sarah shook her head. "But come along, Dr. Morse—Abigail needs you." She led the doctor up the stairs.

When they reached Abigail's bedside, she said, "The doctor's here, Abigail. It's going to be all right now."

Night had fallen, but still there were thunderings from the cannon outside Gettysburg. Sarah stood at the front window, watching the flashes of light far off. The battle had gone on furiously. She had not seen Tom and did not know how the fighting was going. Suddenly she was very tired and could not really care who won the battle. All she cared about was that she had seen Tom and told him that she loved him and that she would marry him someday.

Sarah heard a slight sound and whirled quickly toward the bedroom. By the bed she saw Dr. Morse, holding a newborn baby, all red and wrinkled. The doctor grinned at her, slapped the baby, and a cry suddenly filled the room. Abigail's baby was very tiny but seemed healthy and strong.

They cleaned up the baby, and Dr. Morse laid it in Abigail's arm. "You've got a fine boy there, Abigail! Your husband's going to be very proud of you."

Abigail held the tiny red-faced morsel of humanity. She watched the eyes squint together and the mouth open in a protest. A smile came to her face. She looked tired but very happy. "Thank you, Doctor. Albert will be proud."

Sarah sat down and gazed at the mother and the new child. A smile came to her lips. She was weary beyond telling, but somehow there was victory here. Her trip had not been in vain. The war raged outside, and men were dying, but in this room a new life had just come.

She reached over and touched one tiny, perfectly formed ear and murmured, "He's a fine boy, Abigail."

7
A Hill Like
a Fishhook

The first day of battle was victorious for the Confederates. They had driven the Federals back into Gettysburg. But it was an expensive victory. Many of their number lay dead, and many more were wounded.

A small fire flickered in the darkness, and there Tom Majors sat listening as Sgt. Henry Mapes went over the list of losses in their company.

Mapes's voice was steady but sad as he named them off. "Jenkins, Conway, Lowrey, and his brother Dale—they got killed early in the fight." Then he began tolling the list of wounded, and the crackling of the fire punctuated his words.

Tom listened, but his mind was only half on what he was hearing. These had been his comrades—young men that he had been through many battles with. And as Mapes called each name, it seemed a sharp knife penetrated his heart.

Finally the sergeant ended the list and rose, saying, "I'm going to see about Henry Staples. He took a bad wound to the side, but I hope he'll be OK."

When Mapes disappeared into the darkness, Tom looked over to where Jeff was sitting, silently poking a stick into the fire and watching the sparks rise. "We took some pretty good losses, Jeff," Tom muttered. "Good boys—every one of them."

He knew Jeff had lost good friends that day. He had helped to bury two of them, Todd Mayfield and Shorty Wagner. Both were very young, not over eighteen.

Jeff poked the fire again, stirred it, watched the red sparks swirl upward. Finally he looked across the fire at Tom. "Now none of these fellows will have any life. They should have gotten married and had children—and then had grandchildren." He added quietly, "Todd's folks—this'll about kill 'em! He was their only son, and they're getting on in years. Now they'll never have any more of their name in this world." He threw the stick out into the darkness and said angrily, "It's not right, Tom, just not right!"

"It's war." Tom shrugged.

Suddenly, out of the dark the tall form of their father emerged. He squatted down, saying, "I'm glad you two are all right. We took some pretty bad losses."

After they had talked for a while, Tom cleared his throat. "Something I've got to tell you." There was an odd note in his voice. "When I went into Gettysburg today something happened." He paused, then said, "I thought stuff like this happened only in novels. It was one of the strangest things I ever heard of."

"Well, what was it, Tom?" Jeff probed. "What'd you see?"

"I was headed down one of the streets, and cannon was beginning to knock the town apart," Tom answered slowly. "I saw this woman come out of a doorway. She started down the street, and a shell exploded not too far from her. Well, I went to get her off the street, and when I got up to her and she turned around—I saw it was Sarah."

"Sarah *Carter?*" his father demanded.

"Yes. Why, you could have knocked me over with a feather!" Tom confessed. "There the shells were falling all around us. I knew we had to get out of there."

"What in the world was *Sarah* doing in Gettysburg?" Jeff asked.

"You remember Abigail Smith that married the Munson fellow? Well, they moved to Gettysburg. The fellow she married is gone with Grant and the Union Army, and she's having her first baby. She wrote and asked Sarah to come and be with her, and Sarah did."

"I can't believe it!" Jeff said in amazement. "Out of all the people in this town you run into Sarah!"

"Is she all right?" their father asked quickly.

"She was when I left her. She was on her way to get the doctor, and I went with her to be sure she got there all right. We got the doctor back to the house where Abigail was, and I had to leave to go on with the attack."

Nelson Majors was watching his son's face. "I guess it was quite a shock finding her right in the middle of a battle. I wish she weren't here. This whole town could become a battleground."

"I felt the same way, but she is, and she won't leave Abigail. I know that."

"What else did she say, Tom?" Jeff asked eagerly. "She say anything about Leah?"

"No, we didn't have time to talk much. I had to get on my way. After the battle's over I'm going to try to get back to her though. She said . . ."

"What was it she said, Tom?" his father prompted. He kept his eyes fixed on his son's countenance and then smiled. "Something personal, I guess?"

"Yes, it was, Pa—I mean, Major," Tom stammered. "Well—" he shrugged his shoulders "—she said she cared for me and someday she'd marry me."

"Well, she's never gone that far before. That's good news." Their father rose to his feet and looked toward the east, where the Union troops lay. "It's gonna be a bad day tomorrow. I've got the feeling that General Lee's gonna want to attack at once. Right now, from all the figures, we've got the Yankees outnumbered—for once."

"We'll whip 'em this time, Pa," Jeff said, forgetting to call his father by his military title. "See if we don't."

"We'd better." Nelson Majors nodded grimly. "We're a long way from home, and if they ever get their full strength up and get us flanked, it'd be bad. You boys watch out for yourselves." He strolled off into the night.

It was perhaps thirty minutes later that Pete Simmons came out of the darkness and sat down beside Tom. He said nothing, which was unusual, for usually he was very talkative.

"It was pretty rough today, wasn't it, Pete?" Tom remarked.

Pete did not answer for a moment. Then he cleared his throat and said, "Something happened to me today."

Tom stared at him. "What was it?" he asked curiously. He knew that Pete had been in some of the heaviest fighting and that at one point had been

70

in front of the whole Confederate force charging ahead.

"While the battle was on," Pete said slowly, his brow wrinkled and an odd look on his face, "I didn't think about anything. Seems like a fellow kinda loses his mind. Shells are going off, and men are dropping, and all you can do is run and shoot as fast as you can. Well, as long as that was going on, I didn't have no trouble. But afterwards—"

Tom waited for him to continue, then asked gently, "What happened, Pete? You didn't get hit, did you?"

"No, I didn't get hit by no bullet—but after all the fighting was over, just about an hour ago, something come to me—just come into my mind. Never had anything like that happen before."

Jeff and Tom exchanged glances, and Jeff asked, "Well, what was it, Pete?"

Pete Simmons bowed his head so that his eyes were hidden. His throat constricted as he swallowed, and finally the tall, lanky young man raised his head and said haltingly, "I got the idea that I'm gonna be killed in this here battle."

"Why, lots of us feel like that, Pete. It can happen to anybody," Tom protested.

"No, it's not like that. I've always known I *could* be killed. But this time it was almost like a voice spoke—inside me, sort of."

"What did the voice say?" Tom asked.

"Well, it was just like something said, 'You'll be dead and in a grave before this battle is over.'" Pete swallowed hard again and ran his fingers through his reddish hair. "I—I ain't never been scared of nothing. Always figured I could take care of myself —but somehow this is different." He looked out

71

almost fearfully into the darkness. "I don't know what's gonna happen tomorrow—but that keeps going through my head over and over again. 'You're gonna be dead before this battle is over.' I—I don't mind tellin' you it's got me shook up some."

Tom had been irritated with Pete Simmons and his blustering ways many times, but now all that left him. He had been in many battles and had seen many men show fear. He had even seen a man fight bravely in one battle, then turn tail and run in the next one, which was actually no worse. There was no explaining the way men would behave under fire.

He knew Pete Simmons to be a young man full of raw courage, for he had seen him demonstrate it all day long. Now, however, he saw that Pete's hands were trembling and that something dreadful was happening inside. Seriously he said, "Well, Pete, I hope that your feeling is wrong."

"I hope so too, but I don't mind tellin' you, I'm downright scared."

Jeff spoke up then. "I'm scared too, and I'm not even in the regular army. But it can happen to any of us, Pete. Even drummer boys get killed."

"Reckon that's so—but it never bothered me before."

Tom said cautiously, "I know you don't like to hear anything about your soul, Pete, or about God, but it might be well if we talked of it a little bit." He waited for Simmons to grow angry as he always did and refuse.

Instead the young soldier ducked his head and grew still. He said nothing, and Tom took that as permission to go ahead.

"The Bible says, 'It is appointed unto man once to die but after this the judgment.' All of us know that, I guess." Tom went on softly. "We know we're going to die, anyway. It's just a matter of time and place and circumstances, and if you were home, Pete, you might fall off a horse and die. That's always been part of your life, like it is of mine and Jeff's here."

"I never thought about it," Pete mumbled. "Never been to a funeral. Didn't want to think about it."

"None of us like thinking about death, but 'a wise man looketh well to his going.' The Bible says that too. If you were going to go on a long journey over the ocean, you'd make some preparation. You'd get some money, get some baggage, say your good-byes. You'd do all kinds of things."

"I guess that's right."

"Well, think of death as being kind of a journey. We all go on it someday. You might not go on yours for forty years—but like all the rest of us in this here army, you might go tomorrow. I think it'd be good if you made some preparation."

Jeff sat across the fire listening as Tom talked gently on.

Tom loved the Bible and had memorized parts of it. Now Scripture after Scripture came from his lips. He dropped them casually, not hammering at Pete or threatening but explaining, as he went along, that everybody needs salvation.

"Jesus is the only way I know, Pete," Tom said at last. "He died on the cross for one reason. Not for His sins—because He didn't have any. He died for your sins. And mine. That day I called on Him, He forgave me every one of them. That's what we call being saved." He hesitated, then said, "I'd like to see you saved, Pete. I always have, but you'd never listen."

Jeff added a word. "It's easy, Pete. All you have to do is tell God you're sorry and you want to turn from what's been wrong in your life—and then call on the Lord Jesus Christ. And that's it."

Pete Simmons looked up. His eyes were cloudy. He said, "That sounds too easy. I mean, there ain't any preacher here. There ain't no church to join. I couldn't get baptized—"

"All those are things that can happen and ought to—but God knows your heart. He knows there's no preacher here. And if you're saved, you'll join a church and be baptized when you get a chance. You'll do all those things. But all that comes afterwards. First you have to get saved. Then you can go on and be the Christian that you ought to be."

For a long time the talk went on around the campfire. Several times Jeff got up and replenished the dying blaze so that it flickered into life again.

After Pete had asked many questions, he looked up and said, "I've been pretty much of a rotter. Never told anybody, but I've done lots of bad things. You reckon the Lord would forgive me for all of them if I'd ask Him to?"

"He says He would. 'Whosoever shall call upon the name of the Lord shall be saved,' " Tom said quickly. "That 'whosoever' means you, Pete." He saw tears in Pete's eyes. "I was saved about like this: Somebody was talking to me, asking me about my soul, and I felt bad about my sins. But then he told me I could call upon the Lord and be forgiven, and I did. Pete, the Lord forgave me when I did that. He's been with me ever since. I think right now we ought to do the same thing. Will you pray in your heart if I pray for you out loud?"

"Yes, I will."

Tom began to pray, quietly and fervently, for Pete Simmons. When he looked up, he saw that Pete's face was lined with tears. "Pete, did you ask the Lord Jesus into your heart?"

There was a moment's silence, and Tom held his breath.

And then Pete said, "Yes! I done it! And He forgave me, 'cause He said He would." Then Pete's face was filled with shock. "I don't know how to explain it, but that fear, it's all gone."

For a long time the three sat and talked about being in God's family. Then Pete said, "I don't know what's gonna happen tomorrow. I may die anyway, but I know it's all right. I sure do thank you two fellers!" He got up then and walked away down the line.

Jeff said as soon as he was gone, "That's great, isn't it, Tom?"

"It sure is. I hope Pete doesn't take a bullet tomorrow, but if he does, he knows the Lord."

The next day the attack began again. Maj. Nelson Majors explained to his officers and sergeants what would happen. He drew a map on the ground, saying, "Look! Here's what we're facing." Then he said, "See that long, low ridge over there?"

They looked to where he pointed with his stick, then down at the map.

"Over to the north are Cemetery Hill and Culp's Hill. Way down on the other end—on the south—

are the Round Tops. If we can take either one of those, we'll have the Yankees whipped."

"Which one are we going for, sir?" one of his lieutenants asked.

"There'll be three attacks. General Hood will attack at our far right, General McLaws to his left, and General Anderson to his left. We've got to break that line. General Ewell will attack the other side of the line at Cemetery Hill, but the main attack will be on our right. Right there at Little Round Top."

The attack did not go well. To begin with, General Lee had expressed his intention to strike early in the morning. All of his forces were up and ready, but the Confederate attack did not begin until late in the afternoon.

The key to the entire Battle of Gettysburg may have been the small rise called Little Round Top. A Union general left it unprotected, and only at the last moment were reinforcements rushed to protect this extreme left flank of the Union Army. Again and again the Confederates attacked the position but were beaten back by the furious defense of the Union troops. All day long the attacks rolled. Cannon thundered as artillery pounded both Union and Confederate positions.

It was very late in the day when Tom, thirsty and weary from the hard fighting, rose to lead his squad forward. "Come on, men," he said. "I think I see a gap up there."

The soldiers began to advance, but almost at once one man went down and lay still.

Tom leaped forward, rolled him over, and then cried, "Pete, are you hit bad?"

Pete Simmons had blood on the front of his uniform. He gasped something that Tom could not understand, and then his eyes closed.

Jeff too was beside him in a moment. "How is he?" he asked, nervously peering down at Pete's still face.

Tom held his hand on Simmons's pulse and shook his head. "He's hit pretty bad. Let's patch him up, and we'll send him back to the field hospital."

Tom and Jeff worked as quickly as they could, stanching the flow of blood from the wound in Pete's side. He awoke once while they were doing this and blinked. "Guess . . . I got shot . . . didn't I?"

"You'll be all right, Pete. We're gonna take you to the doctors. They'll take care of you," Tom replied as firmly as he could.

Pete's eyes were glazed, and he had trouble forming words. Jeff leaned forward to hear him say, "I guess . . . it's a good thing . . . I got saved last night, Jeff . . . isn't it?"

"It's a good thing—but you'll be all right," Jeff said encouragingly.

Tom called two men, who carried Pete away on a stretcher, and then the attack rolled on.

When night came, both Union and Confederate forces were exhausted. The Confederate offensive had been fierce, but actually they had accomplished little. The lines were approximately where they had been that morning—with one difference. Ten thousand wounded and dying men were lying on the fields where the battles had taken place.

Tom and Jeff made their way to the field hospital, where they found the doctors still working by lantern light. After some difficulty, they found Pete.

He smiled when they came in. "Hey!" he whispered faintly. "Glad you two . . . are all right."

"Yes, we're fine, but how're you doing, Pete?" Tom asked.

They knelt down beside Simmons, wrapped in a blanket and lying on the ground. "Don't feel too good . . . but I'll be all right," Pete said. His voice was weak and thin, and he asked for water.

Jeff sprang up to get it.

Pete drank thirstily, then said, "Like I said, Jeff . . . it's a good thing . . . we had our talk last night."

"You still know that the Lord's with you?" Tom asked.

"Sure do. Never had anything . . . like this before. I've always knowed . . . I needed something . . . but I didn't know it was God. I ain't never gonna forget . . . callin' on God. I wish everyone . . . in the whole army . . . would do it."

Tom smiled. "Well, when you get better you'll be able to preach to 'em some."

"Dunno as I can do that . . . but I can sure tell 'em . . . about how Jesus came into my life."

When Tom and Jeff returned to their squad, they found Henry Mapes and Curley Henson talking.

Curley looked up. "How's Simmons doing?"

"He's hit pretty bad. I hope he makes it, but I just don't know." Then Tom said, "What's gonna happen tomorrow?"

"I think we're gonna have another run at 'em," Mapes said.

Curley shook his head. "It won't do no good. They're up on top of those hills. We'd have to march right across that open field to get at 'em. I sure hope we don't do that."

78

Jeff looked in the direction of the ridge where the Union army lay. "I can't imagine marching across that field into the fire of the cannon and the rifles of the Union soldiers on top of that hill. They'll never make us do that," he said. "General Lee wouldn't send us into a thing like that."

"I don't know. General Lee ain't been himself this campaign," Tom said. "Pa said he's been sick— got some kind of heart trouble. He's just not thinking like you'd expect Marse Robert to think."

Tom stared up at the low ridge. "Sure hope we don't try to go up those hills!"

8

A Walk into Peril

What's the date?"

Jeff looked over at Tom, who stood in a growth of tall oaks and stared across the open field. "July third," Jeff replied. "Why you asking?"

Tom did not answer right away. There was something almost pathetic about the way he looked out across the field. He managed a brief smile. "Tomorrow's the Fourth of July—Independence Day. Back home they'll be shooting off firecrackers and rockets, and the bands'll be playing."

"I guess so." Jeff did not like the way Tom was acting, but he had noticed that almost all the soldiers lined up in the grove of trees along Cemetery Ridge were not their usual selves. "I wish we were there," he said somewhat nervously. "Back home."

Tom seemed preoccupied with his own thoughts. He kept looking up at the ridge where the Yankees were entrenched.

From where they were stationed in the center of the battle line, Jeff could see the whole fishhook-shaped line of Union troops. Right in the middle was a stand of trees, and they could plainly see the enemy moving back and forth, bringing guns into position and throwing up some kind of breastworks out of logs.

Tom's face was pale when he turned to Jeff. "I just hope we don't have to go up that hill," he said.

Jeff looked at the open field, then up at the Yankee guns on the crest of the ridge. "Why, even I know better than to cross an open field with the enemy on a hill on top of you!"

What Jeff did not know was that Gen. Robert E. Lee had been engaged in a debate with Gen. James Longstreet concerning the wisdom of the planned attack.

For two days, General Lee had sent the Army of Northern Virginia to batter the Union lines. Now he faced General Longstreet, saying, "The enemy was strong on both his flanks, but there has to be a weakness somewhere, and that has to be in the center."

Longstreet looked at the open field, then at the thousands of Union soldiers and massed artillery at the top of the ridge, and said with some heat, "General, I've been a soldier all my life, and I have to tell you that, in my opinion, no fifteen thousand men who ever marched can take that hill."

But for once General Lee was not able to make the correct decision. Perhaps it was because he was accustomed to having Stonewall Jackson present to carry out his commands. Other officers seemed unable to accomplish the tasks he ordered.

Even now the attack had not gone as Lee had planned. Longstreet had moved slowly, and Jeff and the men of his squad had been crouching in a stand of trees all morning while the sun beat down in hot waves.

Jeff took off his hat and mopped his brow. He was thinking about having to march up that hill when he heard footsteps and saw Jed Hawkins approach.

Jed had a strained look on his face as he plopped down beside Jeff. "Well," he said, "bad news."

"What is it?"

"Pete Simmons—he died last night."

The news of Pete's death depressed the squad even more. They had lost many men, and Simmons had been one of their best—a little hard to get along with at times but a good soldier. Now he was gone.

Jeff clamped his lips tightly together, saying nothing. But he was thinking, *Poor Pete. He had his whole life before him, and now he's gone.* Then a second thought came. *I sure am glad Tom and I talked to him about the Lord. He was saved before he died, and that means a lot.*

Ten minutes after Hawkins returned, a terrific roar of guns suddenly rent the afternoon air. It caught Jeff and Tom off guard, and both of them flinched.

Jeff looked down at the Confederate artillery, which was belching smoke and fire. They were shooting as fast as the gunners could reload, and then, looking upward, Jeff saw the shot and shell strike among the Union troops at the top of the ridge.

"They won't be able to keep that up for long. We don't have that much ammunition," Tom shouted over the roar.

He had no sooner spoken than shells began to explode around the Confederates. Although the Southerners were hidden by the line of trees, the Yankee gunners on the ridge began shooting at will. Explosions rocked the earth. One struck so close that dirt was thrown all over Jeff and Tom.

It would be the greatest artillery duel that had ever taken place in America. Cannon roared, shells exploded, and men on both sides were killed and maimed as the exchange went on.

Behind them the officers were running about, getting their orders, when Maj. Nelson Majors came striding through the trees. "Get ready, boys!" he said. "General Lee says we're gonna take that hill! We'll file in with General Pickett's men."

Nelson Majors, like most of the other officers assigned to make the charge, was unhappy. All of them could see that they would have to cross at least a half mile of open field under the guns of the enemy. But orders were orders, and the generals began to step out, calling for their men to fall into battle positions.

The long lines formed. The Confederate guns were quiet. *Out of ammunition,* Nelson Majors supposed. He looked up and down the lines, waiting for the command to go forward. He felt a moment's heart-wrenching fear, for he knew what was coming. Many of these fine young men under his command would be dead in less than half an hour, but there was no turning back. He drew his sword, lifted it, and, when the command came, shouted, "Forward, men. Be good soldiers now."

Jeff advanced, beating his drum slowly, and he heard its drumbeat echoed as drummers on the far end of the company did the same.

Battle flags fluttered in the slight breeze, and unit flags whipped as the soldiers marched. There was a pride in them that caused them to keep their lines dressed and trim, and up on the ridge the Federals looked down with admiration.

"You gotta give it to those Rebs," a Yankee lieutenant breathed softly. "Look at 'em! Coming like they're on a parade ground."

"They won't keep those ranks long," another officer said. "But they do look great, don't they? Never doubted that the Rebs had courage. But they're fools for coming up that hill."

There was no cover whatsoever for the marching columns. Instead there were fences and stone walls that had to be hurdled as the troops advanced. But up they went. Heat waves shimmered on the gentle slope, grown over with ripening grain. Up they went toward Cemetery Ridge.

From time to time those who stayed behind in reserve saw the lines disappear into small depressions, then emerge again, the uneven ground making their march more difficult. Some men were so overcome by the sun that all they could do was stumble blindly forward.

Far down the line, General Pickett watched his men parade across the slope. He was proud of these men, most of them Virginians, and the coal black horse that he rode stamped the earth, excited by the sound of the drums.

Jeff wiped the sweat from his face. His hands were trembling, and his heart pounded. The thudding of his drum seemed to have entered his heart. As he glanced down the line, he saw the strained, bearded faces of his friends, and the hands that gripped their muskets were white. On Jeff went, and it was a strange feeling. Soon, he knew, the bullets would begin flying and the shells exploding.

They're just waiting, he thought, *until we get closer, so that they can't miss.*

Onward he marched. Looking down the slope, he saw Tom, clasping his musket in both hands. His face was pale, but he was encouraging his men to keep their lines straight.

Far off to Jeff's left he saw his father, wearing his best uniform of ash gray, his back straight, carrying a flashing saber. Fear struck him then. *We could all be killed in a few minutes,* he thought, and one of the drumsticks slipped from his hands. He halted, picked it up desperately, then caught up the steady drumming rhythm.

And then the enemy opened up with sudden, terrible musket fire. Men began to fall on Jeff's right and left. A flag went down but was picked up at once by another soldier. He stepped over the body of the fallen flag bearer, and the line moved onward, straight onward.

Cannon began to roar. Grape and canister shot plunged and plowed through the ranks. Bullets whizzed thick as hailstones around Jeff, and he expected to fall to the ground any moment, shot through.

General Pickett moved alongside his valorous troops, as if courting death. He waved his hat, and the black stallion snorted and tore the turf with his hooves.

General Kemper, with hat in hand, cheered his men on. And General Armistead put his hat on his saber and held it high.

Jeff noticed that rabbits, frightened by the guns, were fleeing everywhere. It was a small thing to notice, but he thought, *I'm about as afraid as these rabbits are! They don't know what's happening—but I do!*

Just then a shell struck to his right. It killed men instantly. One man was down, holding his stomach. He was only a boy, and his sergeant and Tom had to restrain others who would stop to help him. "Close up! Close up!" they yelled.

Jeff could see the Yankee batteries shooting. He could see the black cannonballs bouncing along like bowling balls. And sometimes, tumbling over and over in the air, were the men that had been struck by them.

The Confederates reached the road that cut through the middle of the field. There they were forced to take down fence rails. Musket fire now was beginning to reach them, and men were dropping in a long, neat line of dead. Canister, millions of metal balls, whirled through the air. Everywhere men were falling.

Still on they went. They were almost at the top now, and General Armistead was screaming for a charge. There was no strength left in Jeff, but he stumbled onward, close enough now to see the blue figures behind the fences at the summit.

He noticed especially one young Union soldier who looked to be no older than Jeff was. He was drawing a bead, it seemed, right on Jeff, when suddenly a shot took him and drove him over backward.

Then they were at the ridge-top fence line, and some of the company were over but fighting desperately hand to hand with their muskets or whatever else they could find. It was at this moment that Jeff glanced back and saw an exploding shell hurl Tom to the ground, where he rolled over and over.

"Tom!" Jeff yelled and dropped his drum. He ran to Tom, who was holding his left leg. It was crimson.

His brother's eyes were filled with pain, and he gasped, "Go back, Jeff. Get out of this."

"No! I'm not going back without you!" Jeff stood there irresolutely. Then he ran back to his drum and ripped off the cording used to hold it over his shoulder. Blood was pouring from Tom's leg just below the knee. Jeff formed a quick tourniquet with the cording, and the bleeding stopped at once.

Jeff crouched beside Tom, holding him in the din of battle. The field about him seemed covered with the bodies of men. Some were crawling back towards their position at the foot of the hill. Others lay very still in an eloquence of death.

Jeff knew then that it had all been in vain. Too few Confederates had reached the top of the ridge. Now they were being beaten back. He saw Henry Mapes, his face bloody, approaching with Jed Hawkins, and then behind them his father appeared.

Nelson Majors saw his wounded son. "We're retreating," he said. He reached down and took Tom by the arms. Mapes took Tom's feet, as Tom cried out with pain.

"Let's get down the hill," the major gasped hoarsely. His uniform had been sliced at the shoulder by a bullet, but he seemed unharmed.

Jeff followed helplessly, never expecting to make the foot of the slope, for bullets were still flying. Finally, however, they struggled along with others, who were either crawling or being carried, back to the safety of their own lines.

When they reached the trees, Majors said, "We've got to get him to the field hospital. That leg looks bad."

Tom was gritting his teeth, his eyes shut. He opened them now, looked down at the leg, and said, "Pa, don't let 'em take my leg off!"

Nelson Majors stared at the mangled lower leg and said gently, "They'll do the best they can for you, son."

Jeff took one look at his father's face, then glanced at Tom's leg, and knew that there was no hope.

9
Field Hospital

Jeff stood in the shade of the trees, the cannons' echoes still numbing his ears, and watched men stumble down the hill. Their faces were blank, and most had left their muskets behind—thrown them away. He was about to turn and leave the front line when he suddenly saw a man on a gray horse cross the open ground in front of the trees.

"It's General Lee!" The cry went up from the men, and there was a surge of movement toward the white-haired man. He had taken off his hat and was walking his horse slowly along the first rows of dead. He reined up, gazed for a moment at the troops, and was motionless as a statue.

And then the men began coming to him. Some reached up to touch him, and he reached down to shake their hands. As he began talking to them, Jeff saw there were tears running down his cheeks.

"It's all my fault," he said, his voice gentle and pain in his eyes.

The men began shouting, "No! It's not your fault, General Lee!" One of them said, "Let's go back! We can do it! We can whip 'em!"

But General Lee shook his head. "We will rest and try it again another day. Now, you must show good order. Never let them see you run."

Lee rode slowly forward. A hundred or more men gathered about his horse as it picked its way carefully through the crowd.

Jeff turned away, somehow feeling lost and as if he wanted to cry. Many of the men were crying, but Jeff bit his lip and muttered, "No point in that now. I've got to go see about Tom."

He had not time to do so at the moment, however, for there was danger that the Union troops would charge. For the rest of the day General Longstreet and the other Confederate officers organized their guns, ready for an attack. They all stood looking across the field, and burial parties went out from time to time. But no attack came.

Later that night Jeff's father found him. "Are you all right, son?" he asked. His face was grimed with dirt and powder, and his uniform was torn, but he was not hurt.

"I'm all right, but I'm worried about Tom."

"The Yankees won't attack tonight. I don't think they'll attack at all," the major said thoughtfully. "If General Grant was up there at the head of that army, they'd be on us right now. But General Meade's not the attacking kind." He stood thinking of what to do, then shrugged wearily. It was if he finally realized that the battle was over, and he said quietly, "Let's go see about Tom."

Jeff followed his father as they threaded their way through the lines. The Confederates had lost an enormous number of men, some said as many as twenty thousand killed and wounded. Everywhere there were signs of the terrible battle.

When they got to the field hospital they saw the surgeons working by lantern light. Long lines of men lay on the ground, groaning, waiting their turn. There was little medicine, and the opium and other narcotics had been used up long ago.

Amputations were being performed in the crudest way.

Finding one doctor sitting and smoking a cigar between operations, the major said, "I'm Nelson Majors. My son was brought in."

The doctor puffed at his cigar. Its cherry-red light punctuated the darkness. He shook his head wearily. His voice was hoarse as he answered, "I am sorry, Major. I don't remember any names. You'll have to find him for yourself."

"Thank you, Doctor."

Jeff and his father began to search. They found that those who had undergone surgery had been placed in an open space off to the right. Some lay on the ground with nothing under them. A few had blankets. The medical attendants moved wearily among the wounded. There were far too few of them.

"I can't see anything. We'll have to get a light, Pa." Jeff had forgotten completely about his father's rank. It was as if the army were now far away from him. All he cared about was finding his brother.

They found a battered lantern with a little oil, and Nelson Majors lit it. They went back and by its feeble yellow light began looking at the faces of the wounded men. Some soldiers begged for water. Some already were dead.

The sight chilled Jeff's heart, and he thought he'd seen nothing worse than this in the whole war. "How're we gonna get all these men back home, Pa?" he whispered.

"We'll get 'em there," Nelson Majors said grimly. He kept moving along the line of wounded. Then he stopped abruptly and fell to his knees. "Tom," he whispered.

91

Jeff went to the other side of the still form, and when his father lifted his brother's head, he saw that Tom's face was feverish, but his teeth were chattering.

"I'll get a blanket. He's freezing to death, Pa."

Jeff knew that blankets would be at a premium, so he sprinted back as fast as he could to his own unit, where he gathered up the blankets of three men he knew had been killed in the charge. He ran back, gasping for breath, and helped his father arrange the wounded young man so that he would be more comfortable.

Jeff looked at his father's face. It was both stern and full of pain.

Tom seemed to be unconscious. He was thrashing about, however, and muttering.

"He's not good." Jeff had seen that the leg had been taken off below the knee. "But he'll be all right, won't he, Pa?"

"These things are hard. Sometimes gangrene sets in. He needs lots of care. That bandage needs to be changed often." There was tension in Nelson Majors's voice. "He needs to be in a good hospital— but instead of that he'll be thrown into a wagon with all these other men and bounced all the way back across the river." He hesitated, then whispered, "A lot of them are not going to make it."

"Tom will." Jeff reached out and touched his brother's hair protectively, then looked back at his father. "He's *got* to make it, Pa. He's *got* to!"

"We'll pray—but he's in poor condition. If he's already got a fever, I'm afraid he'll have infection."

Jeff sat in the darkness, holding his brother's cold hand. Tom moaned most of the night, and Jeff finally lay down beside him to give him the warmth of his own body.

Dawn came.

Jeff could see at once that Tom was much worse. His father had gone somewhere. Jeff straightened up, his bones sore from sleeping on the ground. Far off he could hear gunfire, but it was not a major battle, he knew.

As he looked at Tom, suddenly his brother's eyes opened.

"Are you all right, Tom?" Jeff whispered.

Tom licked his lips. "Water . . ." he whispered. "Just some water . . . please."

Jeff headed for the farm close by. He found men lined up at the well, and it was almost dry, but he managed to get his canteen full and ran back to Tom.

"Can you sit up, Tom?"

"I think so." He grasped the canteen and drank eagerly, coughing as some of the liquid ran down his chin. "That was good," he said. Tom's voice was thin.

He looked down then and saw by the dim morning light that his leg was gone. The sight seemed to strike him dumb. He stared at the wounded member and then lay back slowly and covered his eyes with his arm.

Jeff tried to encourage him. "You're going to be all right, Tom. Don't you worry."

Tom said nothing. There was a hopelessness about him that frightened Jeff, and he sat there not knowing what to say.

Finally Tom removed his arm, and his mouth was tight with a bitter expression. "You'd better get back, Jeff. There's nothing you can do for me here."

"Sure there is. We're gonna retreat, and I'm gonna see that you get good care."

But Tom knew about retreats. He had seen them before. He knew that the wounded would be put into wagons with no springs and that some of the men would cry to be put out so that they could die without being jounced to death. "I wish it'd hit me in the head," he said. "I'm going to die anyhow."

"Don't say that!" Jeff cried. "You'll be all right."

"I'll never be all right." Tom's voice was flat and filled with bitterness. He muttered, "Go on, leave me, Jeff."

His fever was coming up again, and soon he was thrashing about. Jeff held him still to keep him from hurting his wounded leg.

Finally their father came back. "How is he?" he asked, his eyes on the flushed face of his son.

"Not good, Pa. Just like he's lost all hope."

"He's seen too much. He knows how many wounded men die of infection." He stood silent a moment, then said, "I've got to leave, Jeff. I'll be leading part of the retreat. You stay with Tom. Do the best you can for him."

"I'm not going to let them put him in a wagon with a whole bunch of men."

"You'll have to. That's the only way we've got to get him home."

"He'd never make it. He'd die, Pa!"

His father appeared frustrated. The battle had drained him, and he was suffering the loss of many of his men. He'd already helped bury some of his fellow officers.

"There's no other way,"the major said. "He'll have to take his chances."

Jeff shook his head stubbornly. "I won't let him die," he said. "I'll take care of him."

The retreat was slow to form. Most everyone still expected that General Meade would lead the Federal troops in a counterattack.

The Confederates couldn't know, but President Abraham Lincoln was walking the floor of the White House crying out, "Why doesn't Meade attack? He's got the Army of Northern Virginia in his hand. All he has to do is take it!" He wrote a fiery letter to the general—and then did not mail it. He said to a friend, "How can I know what it's like? I'm not on the battlefield, and General Meade is." And so the letter was never mailed.

The next day the Confederates collected wagons for the retreat. They would leave the following morning.

Jeff stayed beside Tom constantly. There would be no fighting, he knew, so he did not have to be with his unit. All the time he was crying out to God to save his brother's life.

He knew how difficult things were. But somehow hope had come to him that God would help, and he knew that unless God did help, his brother would die. Already several men close to Tom had died, their wounds too severe to permit them to live. The burial parties came and took them away, and Tom watched all this bitterly when he was conscious.

That night Jeff once again stayed close to Tom, seeing that he was covered and that he had water. He tried to get him to eat a little. Tom seemed to care for nothing at all. He would only talk when Jeff forced him to speak, and Jeff saw that he had indeed given up hope.

Looking up at the stars, Jeff wondered at the magnitude of them—how many there were. "Thousands and millions, I guess," he said, "and God made them every one." He was always impressed that God could make so many stars. And then he thought, *God made all those stars, but none of them has a soul like my brother. So God cares more for Tom than He does for any old stars!*

This somehow encouraged him, and he began to pray again, asking God what to do. He dozed off just before dawn and had several strange dreams.

He was awakened by the sound of his father's voice.

Nelson Majors was kneeling beside Tom. "We're moving out," he said. "Time to put you in the wagon with the wounded, Tom."

"No!" Jeff said. His last dream had been so vivid that even now he could remember every detail of it. "I had a dream, and it gave me an idea. I know what to do with Tom—how we can get him taken care of."

"What are you talking about, Jeff?"

"I'm talking about the Poteets."

"The Poteets?" Nelson Majors frowned. "What about them?"

"We've got to get Tom to their house. They'll take care of him."

"Why, we can't do that, son!"

"We can," Jeff declared. "We can do it, Pa. I prayed last night," he cried, and his eyes were bright with hope. "And I asked God to show us what to do, and then I had this dream. It was about the Poteets. They were standing at the front of their

96

house, and they were calling to us. And Pa, they were saying, 'Come to us. We'll help you.' "

Nelson Majors stared at his son blankly. Jeff saw that his father was exhausted and could not think properly. There was the long retreat to be made back to Virginia, and he had no faith at all that Tom would survive. With the fever and the terrible mangled leg, he thought there was no hope. They would bury Tom somewhere along the line of retreat.

Now he stood looking at Jeff and trying to put his thoughts together. "Jeff, it was just a dream."

"No, it wasn't, Pa! I mean—it was more than a dream. Because I looked up at the stars last night and thought how God loves Tom better than any old star. And then I asked Him what to do, and then this dream made me think about the Poteets. We've *got* to do it, Pa!"

Jeff's back was straight, and though his face was begrimed and his uniform in tatters, there was no surrender in him.

"You mean you think this idea came from the Lord?"

"I sure do, Pa." Jeff's mind worked rapidly. "It's only about three miles back to the Poteets' house. If we can borrow a wagon just long enough to get him there, they'll take care of him. I know they will!"

"All right. I'll get a wagon, and we'll see what the Poteets say."

Sarah held up the baby and whispered, "Aren't you a fat old thing?" Then she leaned over and put William Munson down. "Abigail, I'm going over to Jenny's. She hasn't been here today, and she'll want

97

to know how you are. Will you be all right for a while?"

"Yes, I'll be all right," Abigail said. She took her red-faced infant, who was beginning to cry, and cuddled him until he hushed. "Tell her to come and see young William Munson."

"I'll do that." Sarah smiled.

When Sarah left the house she noted that there was no sound of gunfire. She had heard that the Confederates had been driven off and that the battle was over. But she had thought of little else except Tom, and even now as she hurried along the street she breathed a prayer for him.

When she got to the Wade house on Baltimore Street, she knocked on the door. There was no answer, and she knocked again impatiently. "I wonder if Jenny's not up yet," she murmured.

But then the door opened, and she saw Mrs. McClelland, Jenny's sister. There was a strained look in Mrs. McClelland's eyes, and she stood there silently.

"Is Jenny here, Mrs. McClelland?" Sarah asked.

There was no answer, and she realized that the woman had been crying.

"What's the matter? What's wrong?"

"It's Jenny," Mrs. McClelland said. She pulled out a handkerchief and began to sob. "She's dead!"

Sarah stood stock-still, unable to believe the news. She had been so concerned for Tom that never once had she thought of anything like this.

"But I saw her just yesterday," she said.

Mrs. McClelland dabbed at her eyes. "She was making bread during the fighting, and a bullet came through two doors. It hit her in the back." She began to sob again. "It killed her instantly."

Mrs. McClelland related what had happened then. The cries of Mrs. McClelland and Jenny's mother attracted some Federal soldiers. They had taken Jenny's body to the cellar.

"They brought her up this morning, and she's down at the funeral home." She began to moan. "Oh, why did God let it happen?"

Sarah turned away, her heart seeming cold as ice. She made her way to the funeral home, where she found Jenny's body already in a casket that, she was told, had been made for a Confederate officer.

As she looked down at the sweet face, so still, Sarah thought suddenly, *Johnston Skelly will never have a bride now. At least not Jenny.* She did not know, could not know at the time, but two weeks earlier Johnston Skelly had been wounded at the Battle of Winchester. The news of his death would come six days after the Confederates retired at Gettysburg.

She reached out and touched Jenny's sleeve, whispering, "Good-bye, Jenny. You were a friend to me."

Sarah left the funeral home and made her way back to the apartment, dreading to give the news to Abigail.

10

Any Port in a Storm

The sun was midway up in the sky as Nelson Majors drove the wagon down the dusty road. It had not rained for some time, and the wagon wheels sent up small puffs of white dust behind them. Overhead the sky was a hard blue, and there were only a few small fluffy clouds over to the west.

The wheels dropped into a rut, and Tom uttered a pained cry as he was jolted.

Jeff, sitting beside him, tried to shield him but could only say, "We're almost there, Tom. It won't be long now. You'll be all right."

"Where we going?" Tom muttered.

His lips were swollen, and his face was flushed. He had alternated all night between chills and fever, and even now he shivered although the sun beat down on the open bed of the wagon.

Perspiration stood on Jeff's face, but he pulled the blankets closer under Tom's chin. "We're going to the Poteets' house," he said.

He had already told his brother this, but Tom slipped in and out of consciousness frequently and could not remember what was said.

The leg was inflamed. The doctor who changed the dressing just before they left had been apprehensive. "It doesn't look too good. I think you've got some infection in that leg. Be sure you keep it clean, change the bandages. That's about all you can do."

100

Now, as they rolled along the road, Jeff glanced ahead to the white house where they had had dinner only a few days ago. It seemed an eternity ago to him—so much had happened since. What traffic was on the road was headed the other way, south, and when his father pulled the wagon off out of the way of the wounded and battle weary infantry who marched slowly along, kicking up more dust, Jeff thought, *I just hope my dream was really from God. Tom's never going to make it if something doesn't happen!*

When the wagon drew up in front of the white frame house, Jeff jumped out without waiting for his father and ran up to the door. He knocked loudly and, while waiting for an answer, muttered, "I must be crazy. These are Yankee folks. They'll never take care of a wounded Confederate."

The door opened abruptly, and Claude Poteet stood there gazing at Jeff with his alert brown eyes. He ran his hand through his salt-and-pepper hair, then smiled. "Well, it's our young Confederate friend." He turned and said, "Ellie, look who's here!"

Ellie Poteet half shoved her husband out of the way. She was wearing a plain gray dress again, and her hair was wound around her head in a braid. "Why, it's young Mr. Majors." She looked over Jeff's shoulder and saw the wagon and the Confederate officer sitting there holding the lines. Looking back to Jeff she asked, "What's wrong?"

Jeff swallowed hard and tried to find the right words. "Well," he said slowly, "my brother, Tom—he's been shot."

"Oh, that's a shame." Ellie Poteet's warm brown eyes filled with compassion. "And is thee all right, young Mr. Jeff?"

"Oh, I'm fine," Jeff answered quickly. But he could not for the life of him get out what he had come to say. It had all sounded well enough back in the camp. Everything was noise there, and he'd been so confused. He would have grabbed at any hope. But now, standing here in the quietness of the morning and looking at this couple, he felt suddenly that he had done a foolish thing.

Claude Poteet glanced at the wagon, then back at Jeff. "Does thee wish to come in? My wife is a fine nurse. Perhaps she can help."

Eagerly Jeff's eyes lit up. "That's what I've come to talk to you about, Mr. Poteet. But you'll probably think I'm crazy."

There was a little stream of humor in Claude Poteet. He smiled slightly and said, "Sometimes I think the whole world is crazy except me and my wife." He glanced at Ellie and added slyly, "Sometimes I even wonder about her."

"Hush thy foolishness, Claude!" Ellie said. Then she appeared to take in the desperate condition of Jeff's uniform and the weariness and the worry in his face. "What is thy purpose, friend Jeff?"

"Well—" Jeff swallowed hard and finally blurted out, "Me and my pa, that's him on the wagon, we're worried about Tom. He lost his leg, you see, and he's got an infection, and he's got bad fever . . ."

"Ah, the poor lad," Ellie said. "We heard that there were so many wounded that all the houses in Gettysburg are filled with soldiers, and the hospitals, such as they are, are overflowing."

"Well, we have to get back to Virginia. But me and Pa are afraid that Tom won't make it. It's awful hard for a wounded man to ride in a wagon without springs all the way back through the hills. And he's awful sick, Mrs. Poteet."

The couple stood there watching Jeff. There seemed to be some sort of communication between them, although they did not speak.

Ellie asked suddenly, "How old is thee, Jeff?"

"I'm sixteen."

Ellie Poteet's round face suddenly grew sad. "Our own boy would have been just sixteen if he had lived through the cholera. He was not as tall as thee, but something about thee reminds me of him."

"Let us talk to thy father," Claude Poteet said.

Relieved to have some help to explain the situation, Jeff lifted his voice. "Sir, will you come over here?"

Nelson Majors wrapped the lines carefully, then jumped to the ground, his boots raising little dust clouds. He glanced back at Tom, then advanced to the porch. Taking off his hat he bowed, saying, "It's good to see you again. I've thought of your hospitality a great deal."

"Thy boy is wounded?" Claude Poteet inquired. "Would thee care to bring him inside?"

Jeff said quickly, "I haven't told them yet about my dream."

"Thy dream?" Ellie Poteet asked. "What is this about a dream?"

Jeff found it difficult to explain but finally he said, "I dreamed that we were trying to think of a way to get better care for Tom, and I dreamed about you." He looked about and waved his hand. "You

103

were standing right here on the porch, and you were saying, 'We will help thee.' It was so clear! So I thought—"

"Why, I trust we will always help those in need," Claude Poteet said quietly. "What exactly can we do for thee?"

"Well," Jeff said, "I know it's asking a lot, but we don't think my brother will live unless he gets good care. Could you—" he swallowed, then came out with the words "—could I keep him here until he's better?"

A silence fell then, and Jeff's heart sank. He glanced desperately at his father, whose eyes were half closed and offered no encouragement. It was an enormous favor to ask. These were Yankees, not Southerners—and although they were not in the war, they had neighbors who were.

"Well, I guess it was just a crazy dream," Jeff said. "We'll just be—"

"I read in my Bible that God sometimes used dreams to speak to His people," Claude Poteet said. His eyes grew thoughtful, and he turned to his wife.

She returned his gaze, and it seemed to Jeff that the two were communicating again.

Then a smile turned the corners of Claude Poteet's lips upward. "Ellie and I feel that we should help thy son."

"It could be dangerous—you know that," Nelson Majors warned.

"We fear the Lord but not man," Ellie Poteet said firmly. She was thinking quickly it seemed, and she said, "Husband, I think it might be best to put them in Clyde's old room out in the barn. That way, if anyone comes into the house, he'll be safe."

"A good idea, wife." Then Claude explained. "One of our hands fixed a very nice room up in the loft of the barn. He left some time ago, but it's still suitable. Needs cleaning out. . . ."

"I'll do that. And I'll take care of him," Jeff said quickly. "You won't have to do anything. I'll do it all."

"Well, then. Come along with me, young fellow, and we'll go get it ready. Drive your rig around to the barn door, Major."

Jeff had never been so relieved. He tried to thank his host. "I don't know how to thank you for this, Mr. Poteet. It's gonna save Tom's life."

"Why, we're put on this earth to help one another, friend Jeff. I trust thee would do the same for me."

In the barn a flight of steps led up to the loft, where a room had been framed off and even papered. Evidently Clyde had been a neat man, for there was a table, a bed, a washstand, and even carpet on the floor.

"Why, this is fine," Jeff said. "And it's private too. If anyone comes, they'll never know we're here."

They made the bed ready, and then went downstairs to where the wagon was pulled up into the barn.

"Well, young fellow. Time for you to go upstairs." Claude Poteet smiled at Tom.

It took both Jeff and his father to get Tom upstairs, but when they had stripped off his uniform and laid him on the bed, he gave a sigh of relief. "This is good," he whispered and seemed to relax.

His face was still flushed though, and Claude Poteet said, "I'll have Ellie come up. She is a fine nurse."

Jeff and his father watched as Ellie Poteet cared for Tom. Jeff saw at once that she was indeed a fine nurse. She removed the bandage, cleaned the wound, and replaced the dressing with gentleness and firmness.

When finally it was time for the major to go, he said, "Jeff, I'll have to say good-bye. Take care of your brother as best you can."

Jeff wanted to hug his father but felt that wouldn't be fitting—the Poteets were standing beside them.

Nelson had said his good-bye to Tom already, and now he embraced Jeff, holding him hard for a moment. "Jeff, I'll never doubt your special dreams again." Then he shook hands with Claude Poteet and smiled at the short, cheerful woman. "I think you're an angel, Mrs. Poteet. God bless you for taking care of my son."

Then he leaped into the wagon.

Jeff watched as he drove out and joined the line of retreat that was going down the road. He turned then to the Poteets and for one moment could not speak. At last he said, "Well, you've got a couple of Rebels on your hands, it looks like."

"You're looking better, Tom," Jeff said. He took the empty bowl from his brother, who was sitting propped up in the bed, his face seemingly clear from all fever. "You look like you feel better."

"I don't think I could have felt much worse," Tom said.

For two days they had been in the loft of the barn, and during that time Tom had been carefully cared for not only by Jeff but by the Poteets. The warm food, the clean linens, the dressing changes, and the cool baths that Mrs. Poteet had administered despite his protests had worked wonders.

"I don't see how we're gonna get out of here, though. The Yankees are gonna be thick as fleas, Jeff," he muttered. There was unhappiness in his eyes, a shadow that had not been there before the battle. He looked down at his injured leg, and his lips tightened. "I'm nothing but a cripple. I couldn't run if I had to."

"Don't worry about that," Jeff said quickly. "We'll make it."

Promising to be back soon, he left Tom to read one of the books that Ellie Poteet had brought out for him. It was a book of sermons, and rather heavy ones at that. He knew Tom did not find them very interesting.

When Jeff got downstairs, he looked out to the road and saw a troop of blue-clad cavalry go by. He had shed his uniform and was wearing a pair of faded overalls and a checked red and blue shirt, the gift of Claude Poteet. He looked like a farmer. But he was also aware that, the instant he opened his mouth, his Southern drawl would give him away.

He watched the cavalry disappear down the road, sending up huge clouds of dust, then went into the house. He found Ellie Poteet at the sink washing dishes. "Tom ate it all, Mrs. Poteet."

"That's good. Now I'm going to make a pie. What does thee favor, Jeff?"

"Oh, any kind of pie is good," Jeff said. He sat down at the table and watched her, adding, "The worst piece of pie I ever ate was real good!"

Ellie Poteet giggled at him. Although forty-five, she seemed much younger. She had two grown daughters, both married, and she seemed rather lonesome at times. "It's nice to have some hungry men to cook for. Claude doesn't eat any more than a chicken."

Jeff thought it was odd that she was so heavy and her husband was so lean. He thought of the nursery rhyme "Jack Sprat could eat no fat; his wife could eat no lean," and a smile came to his lips.

Claude Poteet stamped his boots outside, then shoved the door open. "How is friend Tom?" he asked.

"Much better, Mr. Poteet. But I'm worried."

"The Bible says, 'Fret not!'" The Quaker sat down and said, "Ahhh!" when Ellie set a glass of buttermilk in front of him. "'Fret not'—that's what it says. What is thee fretting about?"

"Well, we're sort of trapped here," Jeff said slowly. "Tom's getting better all the time, but we can't stay here . . ."

"Thee can stay as long as thee needs," Ellie Poteet said firmly.

"But just yesterday we heard voices in the barn, and I looked down, and there were some men down there. They didn't look up—but what if they had?"

"Those were just hired hands from Toliver's place at the next farm. They came to get some harness I'd sold Toliver," Mr. Poteet explained.

"But suppose they had seen us?" Jeff said. "Think what that would mean. We'd both be on our way to prison camp—and you two would be in big trouble."

They talked for some time, and in the end Claude Poteet rubbed his chin, which still had two days' of stubble on it. "Well, now, I'm not worried about me or Ellie. The Lord will take care of us— but thee does need to get thy brother out of this country—somewhere in the South where he'll be safe."

"The road to Virginia won't be easy," Jeff said.

He knew enough military tactics to know that the Confederate Army had retreated but would be closely followed by the Union troops. Now the roads were probably thick with Union infantry, artillery, and cavalry.

"Tom and I both talk so Southern," he said, "that if we started out, the first patrol that stopped us would have us dead to rights. It'd be a dead give-away, Tom's leg being gone."

"Well, the Lord's hand has been on thee this far," Ellie said placidly. There was concern in her eyes, however. "But thee is right. Your brother needs to be in a safer place."

"But I can't think of a way to get him out of here."

"Thee must pray. Maybe," Claude Poteet said, "God will give thee another dream."

"I don't know," Jeff said. "I know God doesn't usually guide people that way. Besides, I have so many crazy dreams, I just don't trust them."

"Well, the three of us will pray," Ellie said. Then she added softly, "Thy brother's not happy."

"No, he's not," Jeff agreed.

"It's about losing his leg. He feels bad about that."

"Well, I guess anybody would feel that way."
Jeff shrugged.

"I had a neighbor once who lost a leg. It's been many years ago," Claude Poteet said. "It seemed to take a lot away from him. He never got over it, really. Wouldn't try. Just sat on the porch and rocked and grew mean-tempered." He looked at Jeff. "I hope thy brother understands that his life isn't over."

Jeff had been worried about exactly the same thing. He said, "If I can get him out of here, get him back home, things will be better."

"Well, one thing is true. He's out of the war. Thee can't march with one leg."

Jeff thought about that. "As bad as the war is, I think Tom would rather have two legs and risk his life in battle than be out of it like he is." The thought troubled him, and he got up abruptly. "I better go back and see how he is."

As soon as the boy was gone, Ellie said, "It's sad, isn't it, husband?"

"Yes, it is, but God has done a great thing in saving young Tom's life. He's not through with that young man yet!"

11

A Funny Sort
of Dream

Four days went by, and every day it seemed the road alongside the Poteet farm grew more and more clogged with Union soldiers. Jeff kept out of sight as much as possible but peered out the barn door whenever he heard the sound of marching.

"I didn't know there *were* so many Yankees," he said, almost in despair, as he sat beside Tom late one afternoon.

Tom was sitting in a chair, his maimed leg out in front of him on a stool that Ellie Poteet had brought. He looked at it now, his face grim. "We'll never make it back to Virginia, Jeff. If I were whole, I'd try it—but somebody would stop us, and there we'd be."

"Well, they can't stay here forever," Jeff declared. "Sooner or later they're all gonna go back to Virginia or somewhere. They can't keep the whole Union army here in Gettysburg!"

"We might as well give it up, Jeff." Tom's dark eyes were glum and hopeless. "Look," he said abruptly, "there's no sense in both of us going to a prison camp. You can get away. Travel at night and stay away from the roads."

"Let me ask you one thing, Tom."

"What's that?"

"Would you leave me if things were reversed—if I was the one who was hurt and you weren't?"

Tom lifted his head, looked at Jeff's face, and Jeff figured he knew he was trapped. His brother finally said, "I guess not. But it doesn't make any sense."

"The Lord'll get us out of this."

"You still waiting for a dream?"

Jeff had told Tom how he had come to think of the Poteets. He had told him also that he was waiting for some idea for a scheme to get them away from Gettysburg.

Jeff flushed and shook his head. "No, I'm not waiting for a dream," he said, "but I keep trying to think of a way to disguise us so we can get through the lines."

"You can put on a false beard, but you're not going to disguise *that*." Tom gestured at his wound. "A man with one leg—and that a fresh wound—everybody's gonna know he got it in battle. They're gonna know we're not Federals too. You can forget disguises."

"Well, I'm not giving up," Jeff declared with determination. He got up, saying, "I'm going to milk the cows. I'll bring you some fresh milk."

"All right, Jeff."

Jeff went down the stairs, peered out cautiously, and saw that the road was clear. He went to the cow barn and soon had milked two of the Poteets' fat Holsteins. He carried the buckets of milk into the house and was straining it when Ellie came in.

"I'll do that, Jeff."

"No, let me do it. I need to do more work around here, not less."

"Well, thy job is to take care of thy brother right now."

Jeff tried to do all the work he could on the farm, but actually there was little to do right now. The planting was done, the crops were in the ground. Basically it was caring for the animals that took up Claude Poteet's time.

"Hast thee thought of a way to get thy brother free?"

"No, ma'am, I haven't, but I'm not giving up."

Jeff finished the chores, then made his way back to the loft. He took a checkerboard with him this time, hoping to take Tom's mind off his problems.

They played several games. Then Tom said, "I think I'll take a nap, Jeff."

"OK. I'll do the same."

Jeff had brought up a cot for himself, and he lay down on it. His brain was like a beehive as he explored every possible way of making an escape from Gettysburg. He thought of twenty schemes— all of them equally futile. Finally he gave up and prayed, *Well, Lord, I can't get us out of this mess, but I know You can!* Then he dropped off to sleep.

A fly crawled across Jeff's face, awakening him. He slapped at it, muttering, "Get away from me!" then sat up on the bed, rubbing his cheek. He saw that Tom was awake also, but his brother said nothing.

Jeff tried to think of some way to encourage Tom—and himself. He got up and walked to the single window and looked out. "It looks like rain," he said. He was right, for ten minutes later fat drops began to fall. "Well," he said, "that'll settle the dust anyway."

Rain continued to fall off and on and turned into a downpour by nightfall. Jeff went to the house for the supper that Ellie Poteet had cooked. She put the food on a tray and covered it with a piece of oilcloth to keep it dry, and he walked back through the rain wearing one of Claude Poteet's old rubberized coats and a felt hat, pulled over his brow. Still, he was soaked by the time he got back to the barn.

Jeff pulled off the wet clothes and mounted the stairs, saying cheerfully, "Well, here we are. Looks like Miss Ellie's done it again."

Tom's appetite was off, though he made an effort to appear cheerful. He ate sparingly, while Jeff wolfed down his portion. The supper consisted of beef and potatoes and green beans, and there was pumpkin pie for dessert. Afterward they drank the coffee that Ellie had put in a heavy pot.

Jeff leaned back and patted his stomach. "At least we're eating good, Tom. Better than we've had in a spell."

Tom nodded, saying absently, "Yes, Miss Ellie's a fine cook."

Jeff saw that Tom was despondent. "How about some more checkers?"

"All right."

Jeff lit the lantern, and for a time they played, but Tom's heart was not in it. He lost two games in a row, which was unusual, for he was a fine player.

Jeff said, "Well, I guess I'm getting better."

"Guess so," Tom admitted. "Don't think I want to play any more, Jeff."

"You want me to read you one of those sermons?"

"No! They're the worst sermons I ever heard. So dull! I don't think they'd be any better being read out loud either."

The rain was falling now in a steady rhythmic pattern. The full meal had made Jeff sleepy, and he said, "Well, it's early, but I'm sleepy. I think I'll go to bed."

"All right."

"Anything I can do for you, Tom?"

"No, I'll be all right. Go on to bed, Jeff."

Jeff undressed and crawled between the sheets. It was cool in the barn after the hot day, and the rain pattered on the tin roof. It was a sleepy sound, and soon Jeff found himself dozing off. He never knew exactly when he went to sleep, but he slept hard and did not awaken until morning.

"Wake up, Jeff. You gonna sleep all day?"

Jeff came awake with a start. He sat up abruptly and rubbed his eyes. He looked about bewilderedly. "What time is it?"

"The rooster crowed an hour ago," Tom said. He had pulled himself into a sitting position and was staring out the window. "The rain's quit. At least for now."

Jeff did not speak for a moment. Then he said quietly, "Tom?"

Tom must have heard the peculiar note in Jeff's voice. He turned to look at him. "What's wrong?"

Jeff hesitated for one moment more, then shrugged his shoulders. "You know we talked about dreams?"

Tom blinked and laughed aloud. "Don't tell me you've had another one?"

"I always dream a lot," Jeff said defensively, "but this one—it made me think."

"What'd you dream?"

"I dreamed about Sarah."

Tom stared at him. His lips grew tighter. "What about her?"

"I just dreamed about her. That's all."

"What was she doing? What was it about, that dream?"

"It wasn't much of a dream, I guess. I was just thinking last night about all the folks we knew growing up. I dreamed about you, and I dreamed about Ma and about Pa, of course. I dreamed about Leah." He thought for a while. "I dreamed about Esther too. And then Sarah."

"So Sarah was just one of those you dreamed about?"

Jeff looked down at the floor thoughtfully. Finally he raised his eyes. "She was the last one I dreamed about. Seems like it was just before I woke up. But you can't tell with dreams. And she wasn't doing anything. She didn't say anything. She was just looking at me, and I was looking at her."

"Funny kind of dream."

"I guess so—but it gave me an idea. Now I know what to do."

"What to do about what?" Tom asked.

"Why, I know what to do about getting us out of this place." Jeff saw surprise spring into Tom's eyes. "I'm going to Sarah. She can help us."

"You can't do that! You can't get her involved with us."

"Tom, you're older than I am, and ordinarily I'd do anything you said, but right now we're between the rock and the hard place. I don't know if the Lord

116

sent that dream or not. I just don't know why I didn't think of Sarah before."

"What do you think she can do?"

"I don't know." Jeff got up and began dressing. "But I know one thing—she'll want to know about you."

Tom looked down at his left leg and said, "That's all over."

Jeff was startled but did not argue. "I'm going to see her, Tom. I'll sneak into town after it gets late. Tell me again where you took her—the house she was staying in with Miss Abigail."

Sarah was startled by a knock at the door. It was almost nine o'clock and had been dark for some time.

"I wonder who that can be, Abigail?"

"I don't know. It's awful late for visitors." Abigail was in bed, holding William in her arms. "Perhaps you'd better go see."

Sarah walked out into the large room, holding a candle. She put her hand on the door, and then caution came over her. "Who is it?" she asked quietly.

A muffled voice replied, "It's me, Jeff Majors."

Sarah started with surprise, then opened the door quickly. "Jeff!" she said. "What in the world—"

"Sarah, it's good to see you," Jeff said. "I've got to talk to you."

"Come on in, Jeff."

"No, I don't want anybody to see me." Then he blurted out, "It's Tom!"

Cold fear gripped Sarah. She caught her breath, and an awful thought came to her. "Is he—dead, Jeff?"

117

"No, but he's wounded. He got hit with cannon fire on the last day of the battle. They had to—they had to take his leg off, Sarah."

"Poor Tom!" She asked quickly, "Where is he? Is he all right?"

"He couldn't make the trip with the wounded back to Virginia, so I stayed with him. There's a family named Poteet near Gettysburg. They're Quaker folks, and they're taking care of him."

"I've got to go see him!"

Jeff smiled. "I knew you'd say that. He's awful low. He thinks he's no good at all since he lost his foot."

"That's foolish," Sarah said. "He's the same as he always was."

"He doesn't think so. He's kinda given up hope. I thought maybe—" Jeff stopped "—I thought maybe you could make him feel better."

Sarah stared at the outline of the boy's face highlighted by the candle. "Tell me where he is. You know I wouldn't tell anyone about you two."

Eagerly Jeff gave directions to the Poteet farm. "You'll come as quick as you can, won't you, Sarah?"

"Yes, Jeff, as quick as I can."

Jeff sighed with relief. "I'm mighty glad," he said. "I don't know what to do. We've got to get out of here, but the Federal soldiers are everywhere. I can't stand the thought of Tom going to a prison camp."

"No, we mustn't let that happen," Sarah said. She thought for a while, and her face was serious and intense. "You go on back. You tell Tom I'll be there just as soon as I can."

"All right, Sarah. I'm sure glad you're coming!" Jeff turned and disappeared down the steps.

Sarah listened to his feet pounding on the stairs, then slowly closed the door. Her head was swimming with the news, and already she was making plans of what to do.

12

"I'm Not Worth Bothering With!"

Bu Sarah! I don't see why you have to go so soon."

Sarah looked at Abigail, who was clearly disturbed, but she knew what she had to do. Early the day after speaking with Jeff, she'd announced that she felt it was time for her to return home.

As she expected, Abigail began to argue, but Sarah insisted. "Now that the baby's here, you're all right—and Mary's going to come in every day and help you take care of little William."

Mary Munson was a neighbor who had been away for some time. She was the wife of Albert's brother, and she was attached to Abigail. This gave Sarah a feeling of relief.

Abigail argued in vain.

The next morning Sarah packed her satchel and left Abigail with her sister-in-law, promising to write as soon as she got home. The parting was tearful on Abigail's part, and she clung to Sarah, saying, "I don't know what I would have done without you."

Sarah walked down the street toward the railroad station. But she didn't go there. She suddenly remembered seeing a livery stable down on Washington Street. Horses had been tied to the rail. Several buggies were lined up in an empty field.

Her mind worked quickly, and she knew she would have to be very careful.

A burly man with blacksmith's muscles and a bald head met her as she walked into the lot.

"I need to buy a team and a wagon," Sarah said. "What's your name, sir?"

"I'm Lyle Jones." He gave her a careful examination with his light blue eyes. "Well, I've got a good selection. You wanting to buy mules or horses, missy?"

"Horses if you have them."

"Well, I do have a set that might please you," Jones said. He took her out to the feed lot and showed her a pair of chestnuts grazing quietly. "Five years old. An easy pair to drive. I can make you a good price on them."

Sarah was carrying considerably more than enough money for train fare, but she had not planned on buying horses and a wagon. By the time she had completed the transaction and paid for her purchase, she had only a few dollars left.

Lyle Jones harnessed the team and said with admiration, "You're a pretty good horse trader, missy. You ever want a job, you come back here, you hear me?"

Sarah flashed him a smile. Then she climbed to the seat of the wagon and slapped the reins saying, "Get up, there!" and the team stepped out smartly.

She drove south out of Gettysburg, following the instructions that Jeff had given her. She had no trouble finding the Poteet house, for he had described it precisely. Once she did see Union soldiers marching down the road. They looked at her with admiration as they would at any pretty woman, but she had merely driven by, not giving them a second glance.

As she drew up in front of the Poteets' house, a man came out on the front porch. "Yes, miss?" he said, walking down the steps toward her. "Hast thee gotten thyself lost?"

Jeff had mentioned that the Poteets were Quakers, and Sarah knew by the man's speech that that was his faith. "My name is Sarah Carter," she said calmly. "I believe we have a mutual friend."

Claude Poteet's eyes grew small, and he studied her. "What might thy friend's name be, missy?"

"Tom Majors. And his brother is with him— Jeff."

Perhaps Jeff had not told the Poteets of his visit to town, for the man seemed a little suspicious. "What might thy friends be doing here, dost thee think?"

"I think Tom was wounded and needed help, and he found two people who were glad to give it to him." Sarah smiled then and said, "You must be Claude, and your wife must be Ellie."

Her winsome manner won the Quaker over at once. "Get thee down, Miss Carter, and come into the house."

Sarah stepped out of the wagon as Claude tied the team, then followed him inside.

"Ellie, we have a visitor. We're getting to be quite popular. This is Miss Sarah Carter."

Ellie came wiping her hands on her apron. She took one look at Sarah's face, and then glanced at her husband.

"She's a friend of our two guests."

"Oh, well, thee is welcome, Miss Carter."

"Where's Tom? Can I see him?"

122

"I should think so," Ellie said promptly. "Husband, you take this young woman up there. I'll see about fixing a lunch for her."

As they walked toward the barn, the Quaker seemed to be studying Sarah. "Hast thee known the Majors lads long?"

"Oh, yes, we grew up together in Kentucky. Our people lived on adjoining farms." She hesitated, but then said, "My people were Union, but the Majorses were for the South, so they moved to Virginia."

Claude Poteet processed this information. "Thee is far away from Kentucky," he observed.

"I came to be with a dear friend who was having her first child. She was lonely and afraid," Sarah explained.

"Ah, friend Jeff's mysterious trip night before last—I suppose he came to see you?"

"Yes, he did."

"He told thee that friend Tom has lost his leg?"

"Yes, he told me that."

"It has disturbed the lad considerably, but—" he stepped aside to let her go up the steps before him "—I think thy visit will do him good."

Sarah started to climb the steps, and Claude Poteet called out, "Thee young fellows—are thee dressed? Thee have got a visitor."

"Sure, we're dressed." Jeff's voice came down the stairs.

"Well, go right on up, miss."

Sarah mounted the stairs, and as soon as she came to the landing she saw Tom, sitting in a chair, his maimed leg out in front of him. His eyes flew open with shock.

Sarah did not hesitate. She went to him, put her arms around him, and hugged him hard. "Tom," she whispered, "you're safe. I'm so glad."

Tom appeared utterly confused and shocked. "Sarah!" he said. "How did you get here?"

"I got her here," Jeff said proudly. His eyes were beaming, and he winked at Claude Poteet, saying no more.

"You shouldn't have come here," Tom protested. "It's too dangerous."

"Nonsense," Sarah admonished him. She looked him over. "How do you feel?"

Tom shrugged. "Better than I was."

Sarah knew that it was time to face the real problem. "I'm sorry you lost your foot, Tom," she said quietly. She saw his face flush, and he dropped his eyes, unable to meet hers. She reached out and pushed back his dark hair and added quietly, "It doesn't matter."

Tom looked up and said bitterly, "It does to me."

Jeff put in quickly, "Well, now that you're here, we can do some planning."

Tom stared at him. "Planning for what?"

"Why, how to get out of here!"

"I don't see how Sarah can help," Tom muttered.

"I've already solved the problem," Sarah announced proudly, and as all three men gaped at her she said, "I'm surprised you didn't think of it yourselves."

"What are you talking about, Sarah?" Jeff asked. "What's your plan?"

"Well, the problem is that the road from here to Virginia is clogged with half of the Army of the

124

Potomac. They're all headed that way to have a shoot-out, because that's where Lee's army is. And it's not going to get any better."

"That's right," Jeff said thoughtfully. "Washington's so close to here that from now on the road to Virginia's gonna be packed with Union soldiers. I don't see any way around that."

But Sarah had thought this through. "The answer is that we don't go to Virginia."

Tom was still staring at her, puzzled. "But we've got to go there!"

"No, we don't." Sarah smiled. She wanted to reach out and caress his hair again. She wanted to comb it and take care of him, but now was not the time to start that. When they were free, then they could talk. She saw the rebellion in his face and knew how the loss of his foot had hurt him—had stripped him of his manhood, so he thought. Now she said merely, "We're going to Kentucky."

Silence fell across the room.

Then Jeff exclaimed, "Why, sure! We can cut west, get on the back roads—and I'll bet we won't see any Yankees at all."

"That might be true," Claude Poteet broke in. He gazed at Sarah with admiration. "Thee is a good plan maker, Miss Carter. The roads that way will be almost deserted."

"But we *can't* go to Kentucky," Tom exclaimed. "We're still technically in the army, Jeff. They could shoot us for desertion."

"No, they won't," Jeff said. "We've got men scattered everywhere trying to get back. We're just taking the long way around, that's all. We'll get back sooner or later. But now the idea is to get away."

Tom bowed his head, perhaps thinking he would never be a soldier again anyway. Finally he lifted his head. "It doesn't matter. Kentucky's as good as anywhere."

It was not what Sarah wanted to hear, and she was troubled by the sadness and the doubt in Tom's eyes. *He's given up,* she thought, *but I'll change that when I get him home.* Aloud she said, "I've got a wagon and a team. We'll need to fix a place for you to lie down in the back."

"Jeff and I can do that quick enough," Claude said.

"Sure we can," Jeff agreed enthusiastically. "And we can think up a story in case we do meet any Union patrols."

Soon Ellie came up the stairs. "Well, is thee ready for lunch?"

"Yes," Claude said and then added, "Miss Carter's taking our young friends away. They're going to Kentucky—to her home."

Ellie Poteet considered this and then said practically, "They can leave as soon as we cook enough food to last them all the way there. Come now. Time to have lunch."

Ellie Poteet was as good as her word. All the next day she cooked, and the kitchen was fragrant with the smell of roast turkey and frying meat and fresh bread.

At dusk the day following, Tom made his way down the stairs, aided by Jeff and Sarah.

Sarah knew he hated to lean on them, yet he refused to be carried. The trip hurt him, but he bit his lips and said nothing.

126

The wagon had a canvas top and was loaded with fresh-smelling food. Inside was a bed made of straw ticking and clean blankets.

Tom stood behind the wagon and said his good-byes to the Poteets. "I thank you folks," he said. "I didn't know Yankees could be so generous."

"I think folks that know the Lord are the same, both North and South," Claude Poteet said. He took the young man's hand and shook it.

But Ellie pulled his head down and gave him a kiss on the cheek. "Thee has good friends, and thee must trust God to make up thy loss," she said.

Tom stared at her. She was telling him to put his loss aside, to get on with his life. But all he could do was murmur, "Thank you, Mrs. Poteet, for everything." He eased himself into the wagon.

The other good-byes were said. Jeff also took a kiss from Mrs. Poteet and shook Claude's hand, thanking them profusely.

Ellie reached her hands out to Sarah. When Sarah took them, she pulled her closer, saying, "Thee has a good man, but he is fearfully hurt."

"I know."

"I don't mean his leg. He can overcome that. But he is hurt inside, in his spirit. Thee must be very patient."

Sarah knew exactly what the woman was saying. "I know. You must pray for us, Mrs. Poteet, you and your husband."

"Indeed. Thee knows I will do that." Then she said, "Will thee write me a letter?"

"Of course, I will."

"Good. I will be expecting great things from thee and from thy young man."

Sarah flushed. She said quietly, "I love him very much."

"He will need all of thy love and all of God's love too," Ellie whispered.

Then they were all in the wagon. Jeff and Sarah were on the front seat, Jeff driving. He spoke to the team, and they started down the lane.

They looked back and waved until they turned onto the road and the Poteets disappeared into the darkness. Jeff said, "Fine people. They've saved Tom's life."

"Yes, and they're devoted to each other. You could see that, couldn't you? And fine Christians too."

The wagon rumbled along. The moon was full, and the dark sky was spangled with stars, so that the road was clearly visible.

Sarah looked back into the wagon once. She could not see Tom's face, but she whispered, "Are you all right, Tom?"

There was a long silence, and Tom said gruffly, "I'm all right."

Sarah heard the hurt and doubt in his voice, and as she turned back to peer down the moonlit road she prayed, "O God, teach me how to help Tom be the man You want him to be."

13
Perilous Journey

An owl uttered an eerie call somewhere deep in the woods. The yellow light of the campfire made a dot in the darkness.

Jeff watched Tom descend from the wagon after their fourth night's journey, which had begun at twilight. Using the rough-hewn crutch that Jeff had whittled with his bowie knife and hatchet, he came up to the fire and lowered himself carefully, gritting his teeth to keep back a cry of pain.

Tom leaned back on an elbow. He was obviously feeling better now, though his leg still hurt considerably. The Poteets had included some pain-killing medicine along with the food that they had sent along, but it had been only a small amount, and he had taken the last dose yesterday.

"How are you feeling, Tom?"

Tom looked across the fire to where Sarah was putting a piece of ham in the frying pan. She had left her bonnet off, and the firelight illuminated her dark hair. She was smiling at him.

"All right," Tom said. His tone was flat, and he did not return her smile.

Sarah set the pan on some rocks over the glowing coals, and the ham began to sizzle almost at once. "We'll all feel better when we have breakfast," she said. She went over to the wagon and came back with her hands full of eggs. Stooping down, she began to break them into another skillet balanced on the rocks. "It was nice of the Poteets to give us all these groceries," she remarked.

When the eggs began to bubble up, she used a broad-bladed knife to free them from the pan. Skillfully she flipped them over and smiled again at Tom. "You want yours with the yolks runny, right?"

"That sounds all right," Tom said.

Jeff dumped a load of dry wood close by and stood beside the fire. Sniffing, he said eagerly, "That smells good. I hope we've got enough grub left to last us to Kentucky."

Sarah turned over the last egg and studied them. Picking up salt and pepper, she applied both liberally. "How far do you think we are from Kentucky, Jeff?"

Jeff pulled his hat off and scratched his head. "Can't really say, being as we don't have a map—but I figure another day or two we ought to be in shooting distance of it."

"I'll be glad to get there." Sarah carefully placed two eggs on a tin plate. Then she hewed off a piece of ham with a sharp knife. Rising, she said, "Here, Tom. Eat all you can."

Tom took the plate and the fork and began cutting the eggs. After chewing thoughtfully on a bite, he said quietly, "That's real good, Sarah."

Sarah gazed at him for a moment and then returned to distribute the rest of the eggs. "Coffee'll be done in a minute." She sat down and ate slowly, listening as Jeff described a deer he had seen while out gathering wood.

"I wish I'd had a rifle," he said. "I could have hit him easy. Then we'd have had meat all the way home."

After that, conversation began to lag around the campfire. Tom rarely had anything to say.

They had been traveling at night and getting off the road into the woods during the daytime. Two days ago they had heard—several times—what they thought was cavalry. Now, as they were farther and farther away from the road that led to Virginia, Jeff felt safer and more confident.

"Do you think it would be safe to travel in the daytime now?" Sarah asked. "We could make a lot better time that way."

Jeff chewed on his piece of ham. "You know, I've been thinking about that. There's not likely to be any Federal troopers here. I don't see why we couldn't start traveling during the day. What do you think, Tom?"

"Be all right, I guess." Tom's tone was noncommittal. He sipped at the coffee in his tin cup and leaned back on his elbow, staring into the flickering yellow flames.

He had lost weight since he had been wounded, and now the planes of his face showed clearly as the fire reflected its light on him. There was a different quality in him somehow that disturbed Jeff. Tom had always been lively, but now all of the excitement and dynamic life seemed drained out of him. The shell that had taken away his leg had taken away some of his spirit too.

"Well, then," Jeff said with finality, "we'll do it. We've been traveling pretty hard tonight, so let's sleep three or four hours. Then we'll get a fresh start."

They finished their meal, and Jeff went down to the creek to scour the dishes in the sandy soil. When he came back, he saw that Tom had stretched

131

out with his head braced on his rolled-up coat. He was not asleep, however, but was staring straight up into the sky. Sarah was rolled up in her blanket, and Jeff wondered if she were asleep.

He put more wood on the fire and sat watching as the blaze consumed it and it crumbled into glowing ashes. Then he too rolled up in his blanket and went to sleep.

They rose at dawn, ate the remains of the ham, and washed it down with creek water. Tom crawled back into the wagon, and they resumed their journey.

The sun was almost exactly overhead when Jeff heard the sound of horses approaching.

"Listen!" He pulled back on the lines, stopping the chestnuts. "You hear that?"

Sarah cocked her head to one side and listened intently. "I think so. A lot of horses coming, isn't it?"

"Sure is!" A worried look came over Jeff's face. "When that many horses come, it's likely to be cavalry." He looked to both sides of the road desperately. "No place to get off the road here. We'll have to hope they don't stop. Get up, hosses!"

They had traveled not more than a hundred yards when a line of blue-clad troopers appeared over the crest of a hill. There were possibly twenty of them.

A youthful lieutenant led the troop, and as they drew near the wagon, he threw up his hand and cried out a command. The column halted, and the lieutenant advanced with a grizzled sergeant close behind him.

"Hello, Lieutenant," Jeff said immediately. "Nice-looking troop you got there."

The lieutenant nodded briefly. His sharp, black eyes fell on Sarah, and he considered her for a moment. She was wearing a plain gray dress and a bonnet, but her good looks were obvious even in such garb.

"Where you headed for?" the lieutenant demanded.

"Going home," Jeff said. "My brother took sick, and we're trying to get there so he can get better."

"Sergeant, have a look!"

The heavyset sergeant got off his horse, groaning as he did so, and stalked to the rear of the wagon. He lifted up the canvas that served as an apron and stared inside. "One man back here, lieutenant," he called out.

"I'll have a look myself." The lieutenant expertly moved his horse around, leaned out of the saddle, and peered into the wagon.

Jeff glanced back. Tom had closed his eyes and was pretending to be asleep or unconscious.

For what seemed a long time the lieutenant stared at Tom, then straightened up. He brought his horse about and faced Jeff and Sarah. "Where's your home?" he demanded.

Jeff decided that the truth, as close as possible, would be the best. "Pineville, Kentucky," he said.

"Where you coming from?"

Desperately Jeff took a chance. "Near Jessieville," he said.

Actually this was not made up. There was a very small village called Jessieville not far from Gettysburg. It probably had no more than four or five families and one store, but he had seen the name on a handmade sign. "It's a few miles back— way back in the woods," he added glibly. "But my

133

brother, he took sick. Not doing well, either, as you can see . . ."

The lieutenant stared at him unblinkingly, then his eyes went to Sarah. "What's your name, miss?"

"Sarah."

"These men your brothers?"

"No, sir. We're neighbors. Our families are neighbors. I was visiting, and when Tom got sick I decided I'd better get along home with them."

Jeff knew that the lieutenant was in a precarious position. Kentucky was a border state, almost equally divided between supporters of the Union and supporters of the Confederacy. It was almost impossible to tell who anybody was. Jeff and Sarah sounded Southern, but then so did everybody else in Kentucky. If the lieutenant was assigned to be on the alert for any movement of Confederate troops, he was probably bored out of his skull because there were no Confederate troops in this area.

"You run across any Confederates back down the road?"

"No, sir, we didn't see none," Jeff said, which was true enough since they had been traveling by night. "Some of the Rebels in this part of the world?"

The lieutenant shook his head. He appeared somehow dissatisfied with the trio but unable to put his finger on anything wrong. "Well," he said finally, "you'd better get on your way." He raised his voice and said, "Come along, sergeant."

The two of them took their place at the head of the column, and the lieutenant cried out, "Forward!"

The troop advanced at a slow trot, stirring the dust, and when they were gone Jeff said shakily,

134

"Wow! I thought he was gonna get us for a minute there."

"So did I," Sarah said. She turned around. "Are you all right, Tom?"

"I'm all right." There was a pause, and he said, "That was a close one. Maybe we better get off the road."

Jeff shook his head. "No, I think we can keep on. If they were gonna get us, they would have taken us right now." He spoke to the horses, and they leaned into their collars and once again pulled the wagon along at a moderate gait.

They paused to camp at a small creek, where Sarah cooked supper under the shelter of the trees. The wind was rising, and she said, "It looks like it might rain."

"I wouldn't mind a little rain," Jeff said. "It's been mighty dusty." Tom had not yet joined them, and he lowered his voice, looking at the wagon cautiously. "Sarah?"

"Yes? What is it, Jeff?"

"I'm worried about Tom." Jeff rubbed his chin thoughtfully, his eyes troubled. "He's just not himself since he got hurt."

"No, he's not," Sarah agreed. She was busily putting the meal together, but now she straightened up and followed Jeff's gaze toward the wagon. "He's always been so easygoing and cheerful. I haven't seen him smile since that night I came to you."

"It's just like he's had all the life drained out of him," Jeff murmured. "I kept thinking he'd get over it. And he *is* doing better. He's not likely to die of fever. His leg's clean—no infection." He shook his head sadly. "I hope he don't stay like this all the time."

Sarah bent over the frying pan and began slicing bacon into it. As it hit the pan, smoke began to curl up in tiny tendrils. "We've got to understand how it is with Tom," she said quietly. "He's always been proud of his strength. You know that. Think of all the races he ran. I don't think he ever lost a race, did he?"

"I don't remember it if he did. He was always the fastest one around."

"Well, that's all gone now, Jeff. He'll never be able to do that again." Her face was troubled and her eyes cloudy with concern. "There's a lot of things he can do—but right now he's not thinking of that. He's only thinking of the things he's lost that he'll never be able to do again. He'll be able to hunt after a fashion, but it won't be the same. He won't be able to run fast, even if he gets an artificial leg. He'll always be less than other men."

"But he's alive!" Jeff argued.

"I know that—and someday soon I hope he'll realize that God's really taken care of him. But right now all he can think of is that he's not the man he used to be."

Jeff started to say something, then paused. He watched as she turned the bacon over and finally blurted out, "What about you, Sarah?"

She looked up at him quickly. "What do you mean by that, Jeff?"

"Well, I mean, do you feel the same about him now that he's—hurt?"

Sarah's eyes flashed. "What kind of woman would I be that thought less of a man because he had been hurt? I'm ashamed of you, Jeff, thinking a thing like that of me!"

"Wait a minute, Sarah," Jeff protested. "I didn't mean anything wrong."

"Well, I take it wrong," Sarah snapped. "Would you think less of me if I lost a leg or an arm?"

"Why, of course I wouldn't," Jeff protested, "but it ain't the same."

"What do you mean it's not the same?" Sarah demanded. "It's *exactly* the same."

"Well, I know what Tom's thinking, I guess," Jeff mumbled. He cleared his throat and tried to think of how to say what was on his mind. "You're right—between friends, we should never change. But—I don't know—when a man and a woman are courting, a man wants to be the best with his girl. And now he won't be what he was." He kicked at a stick and burst out, "I don't know what I'm talking about. I must be losing my mind." He managed a smile. "I'm sorry, Sarah. I guess I'm just pretty confused."

She came and gave him a hug. "It's all right, Jeff. I think we all are confused. But we have to remember one thing—Tom's got a long life ahead of him, and he's got people who love him." She gave him a small smile. "And I'm one of them. So what we have to do is be very patient and be sure that we show him all the love we can—and show him that he's no different to us."

Jeff felt better. He grinned. "You're some pumpkin, Sarah, sure if you ain't!"

"Well, we're here. There's the house," Jeff said.

Tom had insisted on riding on the wagon seat, saying, "I'm sick and tired of lying down," and for the last half of the day he had sat between Jeff and Sarah. Now as they rumbled around a long curve in the road and the Carter house swung into view, he said only, "It looks good."

Sarah exclaimed, "Look! There's Ma out in the backyard hanging out clothes. Hurry up, Jeff!"

Jeff clucked to the team, which broke into a run, and when they were a hundred yards from the house, Jeff let out a screech that was as close as he could come to what was called the Rebel yell. Then he laughed. "That woke your ma up. She thinks the Rebels are here!"

He pulled the wagon to a stop, wrapped the lines tightly around the seat, and jumped out. Tom stayed in the wagon. Sarah stepped to the ground and stood beside him.

Then Leah burst out of the house and came off the porch, skipping all the steps.

"Jeff! Jeff!"

When she got to him, he stuck his hand out, but she ignored it and threw her arms around him. The force of her greeting drove him backward, and he protested, "Hey, watch out, Leah—" But her arms were encircling him, and he had to hold her to support them both.

Leah squeezed him, then looked up into his face. Tears glimmered in her eyes. "Jeff, I'm so glad! I thought maybe you'd been hurt."

"Why, shoot! I'm all right," he said. He was embarrassed by the warmth of her greeting—but liked it very much. "Are you gonna hug me the rest of the day?" he asked with a grin. "Not that I mind."

He saw that Leah had grown up a little more. It seemed she grew every time he saw her. She was now fifteen and considered almost a woman in the

Southern culture. Many girls her age were already married. She was wearing a light green dress, her favorite color, and it set off her blue-green eyes very well. She did not seem much taller, but her figure was more mature now, and Jeff said without thinking, "You sure look pretty. I've missed you."

Leah turned red and dropped her head for a moment. Then her good humor took over. "You look pretty too, Jeff!" She looked at his tattered clothes, his dusty face, then burst into laughter. "We're the best-looking couple around here."

Sarah watched the two meet, and a smile was on her lips. She leaned over and whispered, "Isn't that sweet, Tom?"

She didn't wait for his answer but turned to meet her mother. She saw her father coming from around the barn. He started running toward them too.

Dan Carter was thin and had the look of a chronically ill person, but there was a happy look in his faded blue eyes. He embraced her. "I'm glad to see you, daughter." Then he looked up and said, "I see you picked up some strays on the way."

"Tom got wounded at Gettysburg," she said and then got the worst of it out. "He lost a foot, but he's alive. We had to smuggle him back under the very eyes of the Union Army."

Tom sat on the wagon seat stiffly—she knew that he hated to have his injury mentioned. His lips were tight as he said, "Hello, Mr. Carter—Mrs. Carter."

Mary Carter had the same blonde hair and blue-green eyes as Leah. "Well, God be praised that you're both safe. And we've heard from Royal. He's safe too. He's on his way to Tennessee with Grant."

Sarah exclaimed, "I'm so glad he's all right! I think about him all the time."

"Well, come on. We'll see what we can do in the way of cooking up a meal."

There was a little embarrassment. Tom obviously did not want them to see his maimed leg. He scooted across the seat, and Jeff came around to give him a hand. Tom hated to take help, but there was no other way. He eased himself to the ground, balanced on his right leg, and Sarah handed him his crutch.

"I'm OK," he said shortly. They were all deliberately not looking at him, but he was embarrassed all the same.

"Well, come along," Mr. Carter said. "Leah, go tell Ezra we've got company. Kill the biggest chicken we've got—maybe two of them."

"Come on, Jeff," Leah said. "You can go with me."

As Jeff and Leah ran toward the big barn, Dan Carter and his wife turned and walked toward the house. They walked at their normal pace and were inside before Sarah and Tom had covered the distance.

"Tom's in poor shape, Dan," Mrs. Carter said. "He's ashamed of losing his leg."

Dan nodded in agreement. "I've seen it before. We'll just have to pray he'll realize that life's not over for him yet. It'll take a lot of patience, I think."

Sarah was walking extra slow across the yard, but Tom's leg throbbed as he limped beside her.

140

She said, "It's good to be home, isn't it, Tom?"

"I guess so."

Tom wanted to say more. Deep down there was the knowledge that he was behaving badly, but he was a cripple. He could not see any way he could ever pick up his life and make anything of it. Now as he hobbled to the house and struggled up the steps, he thought, *I'll never be any good again. Not ever!*

14

Old Friends Meet

Y ou've got a bite, Jeff!"

Jeff and Leah were seated on the grassy bank of the creek that wound in serpentine fashion half a mile from her house. It was midafternoon, and Jeff was so tired from his journey that he had lain back and simply dropped off to sleep.

The sound of Leah's voice awoke him, and he sat up abruptly, staring around wildly. For an instant he couldn't remember where he was. And then he looked down and saw his red and white cork racing madly around in the water and his fishing pole—which he had braced against a rock— bending almost double.

Jeff grabbed the pole and tried to pull the fish in. He came to his feet, his blood pounding with excitement. For one moment all the problems of the war and of his brother and what would happen in the future left him. This always happened when he got a big fish. He seemed to go a little crazy. As he moved down the bank, trying to land the fish, he vaguely heard Leah calling instructions.

"Be quiet," he snapped irritably. "You think I don't know how to catch a fish?" His big worry was that the line would break. He had not expected to catch this big a fish. They had been fishing with crickets for bream—but this was no bream!

"It might be Old Napoleon," Leah cried excitedly, jumping around as Jeff struggled with the fish. "Don't lose him, Jeff!"

Jeff growled, "I won't lose him. When did you ever see me lose a fish?"

The fish broke water, and his heart seemed to stop. It was a huge bass—as big as Old Napoleon. Maybe it *was* him. However, Old Napoleon was the bass that lived in a creek far away, and Jeff knew that this could not be the same fish.

Finally he worked the fish in close and, keeping the tension with his right hand, reached out with his left. He clamped his thumb inside the fish's gaping jaws, which closed on him at once. It hurt, but he didn't care.

With a yell, Jeff slung the bass over his head. It fell to the grass, flopping and twisting wildly, the sun glinting on its silvery scales. Then he pulled the fish along far enough so that it couldn't get back into the water. Finally he reached down and picked it up.

"Look at that!" he said almost reverently. "Why, he must weigh at least five pounds!"

"He's a beauty, Jeff! I wish you could stuff him and put him up over the mantle."

"I think I might do that. He's the biggest bass I ever caught! Look, I'm too excited to fish anymore. You grab those bream we caught, and we'll go on back."

"Do you know how to stuff a fish?" Leah asked curiously.

"No, but you remember Old Man Taylor who lives down the road? He knows how. I think he worked at a taxidermy place for a while. We'll get

143

Mr. Bass there as quick as we can—before he spoils."

Leah scrambled to get the stringer. "This'll be plenty for all of us," she said, "even without that big bass."

They started back across the field, and as they walked along Jeff looked down at Leah. She was not wearing a dress today but a pair of her brother Royal's old overalls. *She even looks good in those,* he thought. *Sure has growed up pretty.*

He wanted to tell her so but couldn't find exactly the right way to do it. Instead he asked her about what had been taking place on the farm while he was gone, about his sister Esther, and about Morena.

Leah was happier than she had been in a long time. She had been terribly worried about Jeff and his family, knowing that they were going into battle—along with knowing her brother would probably be fighting also. Now the sun was bright, the July breeze was delightfully warm and fresh, and the boys were all right except for Tom's wound—and Jeff was back.

She glanced over at him, admiring as she always did his rugged good looks. His hair, which stuck out from under a slouch hat, was black as a crow's wing. He was tall for sixteen and looked maybe even eighteen or nineteen. He was huskier now too. He had been very thin when the war started, but now he was filling out, and his bare arms were brown and corded with new muscle.

"I wonder how many fish we've caught out of that creek, Jeff?"

144

"Aplenty." He nodded with satisfaction and smiled at her. "If you keep on taking lessons from me, you'll be the best fisherman in these hills."

Leah knew that he was teasing, but she pretended to be angry. "I caught more of these fish than you did! I caught eight, and you didn't catch but six!"

"But I caught this big bass, and he weighs more than all those little bream put together."

They argued playfully as they made their way along the path. The sun threw brilliant fragments of light on the pine needles, which had fallen for years, making a soft carpet. Their feet made no noise at all.

When they came out into the clearing and saw the house across the field, Jeff said rather shyly, "You've sure grown up, Leah. You were just a little girl when I left to go to Virginia. Now you're—well, you're a young lady."

Leah might have been a young lady, but she was still easily embarrassed. She felt her face grow pink, and she did not know what to say. "I guess we're both growing up, Jeff. You must have grown an inch since the last time you were here. I bet you'll be taller than your father, and he's one of the tallest men I know."

"Reckon I'll be good-looking like him?" Jeff asked with a straight face.

Leah opened her mouth with surprise, then saw that he was teasing again. "No, I don't think you ever will," she said. This may not have been true, but she didn't want him to grow conceited.

"Maybe I'll be good-looking, and that Helen Wagner will pay some attention to me now." Helen Wagner was the local beauty. She was about the age of Jeff and Leah, and he had felt himself madly in love with her when he was thirteen. "She's still around, I suppose?"

"Yes, she is—and still flirting with everything that wears pants!"

"Well—" Jeff looked down "—I guess I qualify, then. I guess I'd better run over and do a little courting before I go back."

"You stay away from that—that flirt!" Leah burst out. She was not sure he was teasing this time, and she had a vision of Jeff making a fool of himself over Helen the way every other young man in the valley did.

He laughed aloud. "Good to see you're jealous, Leah."

"Jealous?" Leah's eyes suddenly flashed, and she swung the string of fish. "I'll show you jealous."

"Oof!" The fish caught Jeff in the stomach, and the blow startled him.

He looked at Leah—lips drawn together tightly and eyes flashing green fire. "Oh, I was just teasing," he said quickly. "I don't care anything about Helen."

"You followed her around like a sick puppy all the time before you left," she said. She sniffed then, saying, "I trust you've got more sense than that now."

They walked on, silent for a while.

Then Jeff said, "I'm worried about Tom."

"I know. Sarah and I talked about it."

"He's just not himself. I wish he hadn't lost that foot. If it had just been a wound that had healed up, that'd be different."

"He could have gotten killed . . ."

"I know. That's what I tell him—and I guess Sarah tells him the same thing. He just doesn't feel that way about it."

When they had walked halfway across the field, Leah said suddenly, "They're having a dance at the schoolhouse day after tomorrow."

Jeff perked up. "A dance! You remember they had one of those when Fort Sumter was fired on. We were just kids then."

"I remember I had to make you dance with me," she said. She smiled and looked very pretty in the bright sunlight. "This time I think *you* ought to ask *me!*"

"All right," he said, "I will." Then apparently a thought came to him. "That's another thing. Tom was a good dancer."

"If he gets a wooden leg maybe he can learn to dance again."

"I don't think he'd even try. Tom always had to be the best at things. He might dance, but he couldn't be the best."

Leah abruptly reached over with her free hand and took his. "It'll be all right, Jeff. Tom'll come out of it."

He squeezed her hand. "I hope you're right," he murmured, and the two held hands until they got close to the house.

Jeff and Leah showed their catch of fish to the family, and Jeff took the bass down to the neighbor to be stuffed. Leah was in the backyard, cleaning the bream for supper.

In the kitchen Sarah and her mother talked as they mixed bread dough and prepared the rest of supper. Sarah had been strangely quiet since she got home, and now her mother looked over at her and said, "You're worried about Tom, aren't you?"

"Yes, I am, Ma. He's—he's just not himself."

"Well, I can see that, but it'll take a little time."

"I know." Sarah opened a jar of pickles and sniffed them. "These smell good. I remember when we put them up last fall." She took out one, bit the end off it, and smiled. "They *are* good. I love pickles, Ma, always have. I believe I could make a meal on 'em."

"You stop that, Sarah," her mother said. "You'll spoil your supper."

Sarah said calmly, "I'll just finish this one. It's only a little one." Then she looked out to where Leah was cleaning fish. "Leah's growing up, Ma."

"Yes, she is. She's always been such a tomboy. Look at her! Cleaning those fish as well as Jeff could do it."

"Jeff's growing up too. Almost a man now."

"Yes, and I can remember when they were knee high, out playing together in the dirt, fighting over something half the time." A tender smile lifted the corner of her lips. "Sometimes I think of those good times before the war. You and Tom were always playing together, and Leah and Jeff. It's a shame, I think. Of course, we all have to grow up."

Sarah said quietly after a while, "I wonder if all this will make any difference in the way Tom thinks about me."

Mrs. Carter looked at her daughter quickly, her face filled with surprise. "Why should it?"

"Oh, I don't know, Ma. He's just so—so *different*. I try to be just the same, but it's like he's built a wall. He won't let anybody get close. Not even me."

148

"That boy loves you, Sarah," her mother said firmly. "And real love doesn't—you can't turn it on and off."

"That's what I've always said—but if he still loves me, he sure doesn't talk about it or show it."

"He's afraid you won't love *him* as much, now that he's lost a leg. It's natural enough. I suppose most of us would feel like that. We just haven't gone through anything as bad as what Tom has."

"He ought to know that wouldn't make any difference to me," Sarah argued. She was mixing dough now, and white flour was on her rounded arms. She molded it firmly, turning it over and punching it, then finally put it out on the counter and began rolling it with a rolling pin. "A man's more than a foot. Tom's just what he always was."

"Sometimes things happen that change everything," Mrs. Carter said. "For instance, suppose you had a bad accident, and your face was scarred. Don't you think you'd wonder if Tom would feel differently about you?"

Sarah was rolling out the dough and did not answer for a time. Then she looked up, somewhat startled, "Why—I never thought of that, Ma."

"You've never had to think of it. You've always been one of the prettiest girls in this valley. You came to take it for granted. But if you lost that prettiness, I think it would make a difference to you."

Sarah took an empty can and began cutting out small round circles for biscuits, carefully setting them aside one at a time. "I think you're right, Ma. It would make a difference. I'd always wonder if he were just feeling sorry for me."

"Exactly! And that's the way Tom's feeling right now. We've just got to make him see that it doesn't make any difference to us."

"Sure is good to have you here, Tom." Ezra Payne sat down in one of the cane-bottomed chairs on the front porch.

Tom had been sitting there for some time, reading a book. He put it aside and tilted his chair back against the wall of the house.

"It's good to be back, Ezra," he said briefly. He liked this young man a great deal.

Ezra, of course, had been in the Union Army, but only briefly. Ever since he had escaped from Belle Isle Prison and Leah had brought him here, he had stayed to work the farm. He was an average young man in most ways. He had fine brown eyes and very good teeth but was not at all handsome. He was strong, however, and always cheerful.

Now Ezra pulled a pocketknife out of his hip pocket, opened it, removed a cedar stick from his other pocket, and began peeling long slender shavings off it.

Tom watched the keen blade pare away the curving strips of cedar and asked, without much curiosity, "What're you making?"

"Shavings." Ezra grinned at him. He peeled off another shaving. "Just like to see 'em curl up. Smells good too. Cedar's about the best-smelling wood there is, I think." He pared away a few more and then said, "That battle at Gettysburg was pretty bad, I guess. Papers say it was the worst of the whole war."

"It was pretty bad," Tom said. He did not want to talk about the war. He wanted to shut it out of his mind, but always there was his leg that ended just below his knee in an ugly stump, and he realized he would never be able to forget the war. He had a perpetual reminder.

As if reading his mind, Ezra said slowly and carefully, "You know you were lucky in a way that that shell didn't do worse."

Tom's head jerked up, and his eyes grew hard. "What do you mean *worse!* Isn't it bad enough to lose a leg?"

Ezra said apologetically, "Well, of course, it'd been better not to get hurt at all. But what I meant was, it would have been a lot worse if you had lost that leg above the knee." He peeled off another two or three strips of curling cedar. "Quite a few fellows have come back that lost a leg above the knee. Not much to be done about that. But below the knee— you know there's such a thing as an artificial leg."

"They're no good."

"Why, I don't think you ought to say that so quick, Tom," Ezra protested. "I've been thinking on it a lot. You know, I ain't much good on most things, but I guess when it comes to making things out of wood, I'm as good as anybody."

This was true enough. Ezra's talent seemed to lie in woodworking. He had a particular genius for it, and already the house was becoming filled up with beautiful furniture he had built. He did not have many tools, but those few he had he used expertly. He'd put together a shop in a shed close to the barn, and neighbors were coming now, asking him to build special furniture for them. And Dan Carter had said, "You ought to leave being a farmhand and set up a furniture shop. You're a genius with wood, Ezra."

151

Ezra said guardedly, "I don't think it'd be as hard to make an artificial foot as it would be to make a mortise and tenon joint or maybe a dovetail section for a drawer. I figured out what kind of wood would be good." He held up the cedar stick. "Look at this! See how light it is. Take a piece of oak—would weigh probably two or three times this much. But cedar's real light, and you could hollow some of it out. It wouldn't weigh anything at all." He paused, seeing that Tom had turned his head and was looking away.

Tom listened for a while longer as Ezra talked about the possibilities of an artificial leg, then stood up and seized his crutch. "I don't want to talk about it, Ezra. I appreciate your thoughts—but just don't tell me about it anymore."

After Tom thumped off into the house, Ezra sat on the porch, shaking his head. "He sure is sensitive, and that's a shame. I could do him a real job with one of them wooden legs."

Later, Ezra talked to Sarah about Tom and what could be done for him.

She suddenly said, "Ezra, you remember Gus Springer, who lives in Pineville?"

"Sure, I know Gus. Hey! He's got an artificial foot, hasn't he? Lost his leg in a train wreck. He does so good," he said, "I forget he's got one of those."

Sarah nodded slowly, as though an idea was forming in her mind.

Two days after their conversation, a wagon drew up in front of the Carter house, and a man got out. He mounted the steps quickly and knocked on the door.

Sarah answered his knock. "Mr. Springer!" she said. "You got my note!"

"Sure did, Miss Sarah."

Springer was a small man, no more than five seven or eight, who ran a tanning business. He was wearing a natty suit of blue serge, and when he removed his hat, he revealed a shock of rusty red hair. His blue eyes sparkled as he said, "Don't get an invitation from attractive young ladies to come calling very often. Mrs. Springer was a little bit worried about it."

"Come in, Mr. Springer," she said. "I guess Mrs. Springer wasn't too jealous. She let you come."

"When she read your letter, she said it was OK."

Sarah's note had explained Tom's injury and asked him to come out and talk.

He appeared glad to do so.

"Sorry to hear about Tom," he said, "but I'm glad he wasn't hurt worse."

"It's bad enough—or so he thinks, Mr. Springer."

"Well, I can understand that. I guess I thought the world had come to an end when I lost my leg, but—" he shrugged his trim shoulders "—I hardly even miss it now."

Eagerly Sarah said, "It would be so good if you could talk to Tom."

"Sure. Where is he?"

"I think he's in his room. It's down the hall, to the back—I'll go get him, though."

Springer was sitting on the horsehair couch and looking at a magazine when Sarah came back, Tom thumping on his crutch behind her.

153

Springer stood up at once. "Hello, Tom," he said cheerfully. "Glad to see you." He went over and shook Tom's hand. "Sorry about your bad luck, but I'm glad you made it alive."

"Thanks, Mr. Springer." Tom looked at him with a question in his eye and said, "You just out visiting?"

Sarah had not told Tom the purpose of Gus Springer's visit.

"Sure, that's it," he said easily. "But now that I'm here, I might as well give you my testimony."

"Your testimony?"

To Tom this would mean a Christian testimony, but Sarah knew this was not what Springer had on his mind.

"What do you mean 'testimony'?"

"Look at this, Tom." Springer suddenly began dancing about. He moved quickly with ease, ended with a fancy spin, and said, "How do you like that?"

"Why—I guess it's all right," Tom said, bewildered.

And then Springer reached down with his closed fist and tapped the side of his lower leg. It made a solid knocking sound, and Tom blinked with surprise.

Springer grinned. "That's right! Lost my leg right below the knee in a railroad accident while you were gone. Just wanted to come by and show you what they can do about these things." He nodded cheerfully. "I know it's been a blow, but you get you one of these legs." He pulled up his pant leg and showed Tom the polished wooden leg. "Here, let me show you how it fastens on."

Tom glanced over at Sarah, who was looking on with interest. He said, "No, thanks, Mr. Springer. I don't think I want to know."

He was behaving badly again, but she saw that somehow he was embarrassed by the scene.

"Thanks for coming by. I appreciate it." He turned and thumped off. A door slammed.

Springer turned to face Sarah. "Well, he's a little sensitive right now, but he'll get over it."

Sarah was terribly disappointed, though she tried to hide it. "Thank you, Gus, for coming. I think it'll be a while before he'll be willing to listen."

Springer said encouragingly, "Sure, he'll come out of it."

When he'd said his good-byes and left the house, Sarah knocked on Tom's door.

"Come in." The answer was rather gruff, and when she stepped inside, Tom, standing by the window balanced on his crutch, turned to her. He said stiffly, "Sarah, I'd appreciate it if you didn't meddle in my business anymore."

"Tom—"

"You just don't know what it's like, and you'll never know what it's like. Now, if you don't mind, I'd rather be alone. Just leave me alone. That's all I ask." He turned to stare again out the window, his back rigid.

Sarah stood there, terribly hurt. She left the room, and tears rose in her eyes. They trickled down her cheeks. She wiped them with a handkerchief and whispered, "He's not himself. He's got to learn that he's still a man."

15
Another Good-bye

J eff had been struggling for a few days with a problem that would not go away. Leah must have noticed that he had grown quieter, because one day when they were walking alone through a field she asked abruptly, "Is something wrong, Jeff?"

"Wrong? Why, no. I don't reckon there is." He hesitated, then said, "Look! Remember that tree? That's where we found the woodpecker egg we looked for for so long."

Leah fixed her eyes on the huge towering oak. "I remember," she said. "We must have looked for two years for one of those. I still have it, Jeff. Never did find the kingfisher's egg, though. I don't know where they nest."

The two had hunted birds' eggs for as long as either of them could remember. Leah kept them all carefully labeled in small flat boxes in her bedroom. Birds' egg hunting with Jeff was among the most precious memories of her childhood. "I wonder if we'll ever finish making that collection."

Jeff looked at her quickly. Her face was troubled, and he turned her around to face him. "I *have* been struggling with a problem, Leah. You're right." He grinned faintly. "You know me pretty well, I guess. Can't hide anything from you."

"What's the matter, Jeff?"

"Well, I've got to go back to my unit. Tom's all right now, and Pa'll be worried about us."

"You wrote him, didn't you?"

"Yes, I did, but I've got to get back to the army. It won't be long before I'll be old enough to be in the regular army. I'm tired of banging on that old drum anyway."

Troubled light came to Leah's greenish eyes, and she bit her lower lip. "I wish you didn't have to go back."

"So do I. Nothing I'd like better than just to stay here and hunt and get a farm somewhere." He tried to summon a grin. "And hunt eggs and fish with you. Just like we've always done."

A flight of blackbirds sailed overhead, making their raucous cries, but the two did not look up. The birds swarmed and hovered, then fled in a dark cloud toward the north.

"I guess we spend a lot of our time saying good-bye. Well—" Jeff shrugged "—we'd better get back. I've got to talk to Tom."

They made their way back to the house, and Jeff found Tom sitting out in the blacksmith shop. His crutch lay to one side, and he was watching Ezra shoe a horse.

Jeff leaned against a stall and watched as Ezra set the last nails, clenched them, and then lowered the horse's hoof.

Looking up, Ezra said, "I've learned a lot about shoeing horses since I've been here. Mr. Gallion down the road, he's taught me quite a bit. Got a lot to learn though." He took the horse's bridle and walked toward the door, calling back, "I'll see you fellows later. I've got to go feed the hogs."

As soon as he was out of the barn, Jeff ambled over to his brother and sat down on an upturned bucket. "Tom," he said, "I've got to get back to Virginia."

"I guess it's time we went back," Tom muttered.

"I don't think you ought to go," Jeff said. "Your leg's not completely healed, and you'll get better care here than back there."

"What you mean is, there's no place there for me to go," Tom said sharply.

"No, I didn't mean that."

"Well, it's true enough." Tom had not shaved for three days, and his black stubble of whiskers gave him a rough look. He'd always been neat and careful in his dress, but he'd let that slide since he had been wounded. He stared moodily at Jeff. "One place's about like another. Might as well stay here and be a freeloader with the Carters."

Jeff started. "Why, they don't think of you like that, Tom!"

"They should. I sit around eating their food and doing no work."

Jeff wanted desperately to say, "If you'd get an artificial leg and learn to use it, you could do most anything you wanted to." He knew, however, that Tom was mindlessly stubborn about this. It was as if he had made up his mind not to do anything to help himself.

Jeff sat there helplessly. "Well, you'll be better in a few weeks. Maybe the war'll be over by then. I hope so."

"It won't be over till everybody in the South is dead. Never should have started that war in the first place."

It was a bitter remark and the first time Tom had ever spoken in such a fashion. Jeff knew then how depressed his brother was and desperately

158

yearned to say something to encourage him. "Well," he said, "I'll tell Pa your leg's healing real good and that you'll be on your feet in no time." He bit his lip as soon as he'd said that, knowing Tom would pick up on it.

"No, I won't be on my *feet* in no time." Tom rose and snatched his crutch from where it leaned against the stall and hobbled out of the barn. "You go on back. I might as well stay here as anything else."

Jeff knew he couldn't leave it like that. He got up quickly and followed. "Wait a minute." He caught Tom's arm and turned him around. He swallowed hard and said, "Tom, I reckon you know how much I've always thought of you. Never thought more of anyone. But I'm going to have to say something to you."

"Preach me a sermon, is that it?" Tom glared fiercely at him.

"Call it anything you want," Jeff said. He lifted his chin and met Tom's eyes defiantly. "When you went up that hill along with the rest of us, you were a real man. But now that you've had a little tough luck, you've quit. I know it's tough. A fellow doesn't have to lose a leg himself to know how his brother must feel. But I'm telling you, you're not taking this thing right."

"How should I take it? You want me to whistle a tune?"

"I want you to take it like Pa would take it. You think he'd quit if he got shot and lost a leg or arm? You know he wouldn't."

Tom lowered his head and stared at the ground. It had never been his way to let anger rule over his spirit, but now he could not seem to help it. Finally he lifted his head and met Jeff's eyes. "You're right about Pa, but I'm just not the man he is. Don't reckon many men are." He added, "I'm sorry to be such a puppy about this, but I just can't whip it, Jeff."

The last words were spoken in a plaintive tone, and Jeff stepped over and hugged Tom's shoulders. He was almost as tall as his brother now, and the two looked much alike.

Jeff whispered, "It's all right. It's tough now, but you've got people that love you. One of these days I'm gonna see you ride a horse, hunt, and dance a jig. See if I don't. No sermons," he said quickly. He turned and walked quickly away, unable to face his brother anymore. If he had stayed longer, he might have shown himself to be a baby.

"I love Tom so much," he said later to Mrs. Carter. She had come into his room where he was packing his few things, and he'd told her about his confrontation with Tom. "I don't want to be hard on him. I guess I'd be even worse if it had happened to me. But he's got to pull out of it."

"We'll just have to pray that God'll do a work in Tom's heart, and I'm believing that He will." Mrs. Carter spoke softly, and there was a warmth of affection in her eyes.

Jeff and Tom were like her sons, he knew. They had grown up with her boy, Royal, and Tom was only one year younger than he was.

Jeff was heartened by what she said. "All right. I'll believe with you." He looked at his bag. "I guess this is everything. I'll be ready to go first thing in the morning."

"Well, come on downstairs. I've got a farewell supper for you. I want to fill you up before I send you back to your father."

Supper time was filled with nostalgia. All were aware that Jeff would be leaving. He spent a great deal of the time with Esther. He even held her while he ate, letting her taste mashed potatoes from his spoon. She was growing, was crawling, even walking a few steps now. He smoothed her blonde hair and said, "Your daddy's gonna want to see you. I wouldn't be surprised if he didn't get a leave and come."

Morena was standing close by. Her eyes were as blue as the baby's and her hair just as blonde. Jeff reached over and pinched her cheek, and she smiled at him and patted his hand.

After supper Jeff and Leah went out on the porch to watch the fireflies. He planned leaving before dawn the next day and had said his good-byes to everyone else. Now he turned to her as they sat on the steps. "Guess I'll say good-bye tonight. I'm leaving early."

"No, I'll get up and fix your breakfast," Leah said firmly.

"You don't have to do that!"

"Yes, I do."

Jeff felt good about that. He said, "Well, you always were stubborn. Never could do a thing with you when you made your mind up."

"I'm firm. *You're* stubborn!" Leah smiled. She reached out suddenly, took his hand, and held it with both of hers.

They sat quietly on the steps, saying nothing. From far away the cry of a coyote sounded forlorn and lonesome as it always did.

161

"Sounds kinda like I feel," Jeff admitted. He was very conscious of his hand being held. He squeezed hers and said, "I wish I didn't have to go, but I do."

"I know, Jeff."

After another five minutes, Jeff got up. Leah stood with him. The moonlight bathed her smooth cheeks with its beams, and he reached out and touched her hair. "You sure do have pretty hair. You and Morena and Esther—three mighty pretty girls." He turned to go in.

"Jeff, be careful. Don't let anything happen to you."

He gave her a crooked grin. "Don't worry. You'll have to put up with me for a long time."

The next morning Leah was up before Jeff, and when he came into the kitchen he found her already fixing breakfast. No one else was up. She made pancakes and grits and biscuits for him and packed an enormous lunch for him to take on the train.

He had made arrangements to ride into town and let Ezra pick up the horse later. After breakfast Leah followed him outside.

Jeff turned suddenly and kissed her on the cheek. Then, without a word, he swung into the saddle and kicked the horse in the side. As the mare galloped out of the yard, he cried out, "Good-bye Leah! Good-bye . . ."

Leah stood in the yard long after he had disappeared around the curve in the road. Then she turned and went back into the house. She sat down in a chair and stared into space for a while, then prayed, "Lord, don't let anything happen to him—please!"

16
Needed:
One More Miracle

Jeff arrived back in Richmond the first week in August. He went at once to the camp, where he found his father seated in front of his tent, working at his portable desk.

At first Nelson did not recognize his son, for Jeff was wearing a pair of brown britches and a checked shirt instead of his uniform. But when the boy lifted his head and peered out from under his slouch hat, the older man jumped up from his chair.

"Jeff!"

He ran to his son and put out his hand but refrained from hugging him, knowing it would embarrass him in public. He felt a wave of relief. "I'm glad to see you, son. Come on, sit down and tell me everything."

Jeff took a seat in the camp chair across from his father's and looked around. "What's happening? Getting ready for another battle?"

"It won't be long," the major said, his face turning grim. "And the lines are mighty thin. We left some mighty good men back there at Gettysburg."

"How many'd we lose?"

"Best as we can tell, nearly four thousand men killed. About eighteen thousand wounded and another five thousand missing."

"What about the Union?"

"About the same—but it's different with them. They can replace the men they lost—already have, I guess. With us, there's just a gap. Every one of us has to fight just that much harder." Nelson Majors shook his head. "Well, tell me what's happening. How's Esther?"

"Growing like a weed, Pa." Jeff smiled. "She looks like Ma. You've got to go see her." He frowned. "I know you can't right now, but soon as you can, you've got to go."

The major knew there was little chance that he would be taking a furlough, but he said as cheerfully as he could, "Yes, I'll do what I can. Now, tell me about Tom. How is he? I got your letter, and you weren't very cheerful. Is the leg giving him problems?"

"No, the wound's healed up, but something's happened to him inside." Jeff went on to explain how Tom seemed to have given up hope. He ended by saying, "Sarah loves him just like she always did, but it seems like Tom just won't let anybody close to him."

Nelson Majors leaned back in his chair, his brow furrowed. All around them men were active. Horses dragged a caisson and a piece of artillery by, raising dust in the afternoon air, and he watched it all without seeing them. Turning back to Jeff, he said, "I've seen it happen before, Jeff. I think that's what happened to General Ewell."

"What do you mean?"

"Well, General Ewell was a good general—a real fighting man—but he got his leg shot off. He got an artificial one, but then he was thrown into Stonewall Jackson's place. I don't know—those big wounds, they do things to a man. Of course, I never had one, so I can't say for sure. But Ewell just wasn't the general at Gettysburg that he had been at one time—and I think Tom may be the same."

"He'll be all right in time, though," Jeff said. "He's got to be."

"I'm believing that he will. Now then, tell me everything else. I don't suppose you got to see Leah, did you?" Nelson's eyes twinkled, and Jeff flushed. The major chuckled. "I shouldn't be teasing you like that. Is she as pretty as ever?"

"Oh, she looks all right."

Nelson Majors laughed aloud. "She looks all right, huh? That's all?"

"Well—" Jeff cleared his throat "—better than average."

His father laughed even louder. "There was another young lady here looking for you not long ago—day before yesterday, I think."

"A young lady?"

"Lucy Driscoll. Her father was here to visit his brother-in-law. He's an officer in the Third Brigade. He brought Lucy by to ask about you. Said to be sure to have you come and take dinner as soon as you got back. I expect you'd better do that before you put on your uniform again. May not be much chance later."

"I guess I should. The Driscolls are nice folks."

Nelson grinned. "Are you going to write Leah and tell her about all this visiting with pretty young girls?"

"Oh, Pa, don't tease me," Jeff said abjectly.

His father stopped the teasing. "You go on, and we'll see if we can get you a new uniform. You go see Miss Lucy. Go out and visit Uncle Silas for a day. I'd like to get a report on him. When you come back, you and I'll go into Richmond and do a little celebrating."

Jeff's father managed to get him a new uniform before he went to visit Lucy after all. It was ash gray with brass buttons, and the tailor cut it just to fit.

Then, smartly dressed, Jeff went just outside Richmond to the Driscoll place. He found Lucy very glad to see him, and all the family listened at the dinner table that night as he told of the Battle of Gettysburg.

Afterward, he and Lucy walked outside in the garden.

She clung to his arm. "Jeff! It must have been awful—everybody dying all around you!"

Jeff thought about the battle and said abruptly, "It was bad enough. I don't really like to think about it."

"Of course not. Well—" she smiled at him prettily "—tell me about Tom, then, and—you took him to the Carters' in Kentucky? How was Sarah—and Leah?"

"Oh, they're both fine, and my sister, Esther, she's growing so fast."

When it was time for Jeff to go, Lucy said, "It's Cecil Taylor's birthday next week. He'll be sixteen. You'll have to come. He thinks a lot of you, Jeff."

"I'll come if I can. Don't know what duty I'll have." Then Jeff said awkwardly, "Well, I'm glad to be back. I'm glad to see you again, Lucy."

Lucy leaned forward and whispered, "You come back every time you can, you hear?"

Jeff's squad was glad to see him—miraculously, they had all survived the battle—and Curley Henson grinned as Jeff walked in wearing the new uniform. "Well," he said, "you look mighty good there, Jeff. That suit looks good enough to be buried in."

"Oh, shut up, Curley," Jed Hawkins said. He was leaning back, playing his guitar, and he grinned at Jeff. "How's Tom?"

"His leg's healing good, but he's kinda down in the mouth about losing it."

Henry Mapes heard this as he strolled by. "Well," he said, "at least he won't have to fight in any more battles. That's something."

Jeff shook his head. "I don't think that makes Tom very happy."

Later on he had time to talk to his father. They went into Richmond, where they had dinner at a café. After they had given their order, Jeff asked suddenly, "What do you think we'll do after the war, Pa?"

Nelson Majors leaned back in his chair and toyed with the salt shaker. Then he looked up, his dark eyes thoughtful. "I'd like to go back to Kentucky."

"Not stay here in Virginia?"

"No, this isn't home anymore. Kentucky's where my heart is."

Jeff was pleased. "I'd hoped you'd say that, Pa. Nothing I'd like to do more than to go back to that place."

Nelson studied his son. "Jeff, it won't be like it was. Things change. Like Leah," he observed. "You can't go back and be a little boy and girl hunting birds' eggs. You're already sixteen, she's fifteen. By the time the war's over, even if it only lasts two more years, you'll be full-grown, and she'll be a young woman."

167

Jeff remembered how attractive Leah had been and said quietly, "I know things can't stay the same, and I don't guess I'd want them to. You have to go on with life, don't you, Pa?"

"That's right. And it's going to be hard for the South, no matter what happens. It'll take good strong young men like you—and strong young women like Leah—to build it up again. We've lost the best of our young men—a whole generation." Sadness came to his voice, but he shook it away. "Tell me again about what you did in Kentucky. Was the old homestead the same? Did you go there?"

The major watched Jeff's face as he talked animatedly about the place where he had grown up.

Suddenly Jeff stopped, surprised at himself, and said, "I'm talking a lot, aren't I, Pa?"

"You keep on talking, son," Nelson Majors said quietly. "I like to hear it, and one of these days we'll not just talk about Kentucky—we'll go back there, and then we'll be home!"

They sat for a long while, speaking of old times and dreaming of the days to come. Far away a bugle sounded, thin and clear. Hearing it, Jeff blinked, then rose. "Well, we've got some soldiering to do first, I reckon—but someday we'll go back. All we need is one more miracle!"